Vincentia Schroeter, Margit Koemeda-Lutz (Eds.)
Bioenergetic Analysis 2011 (21)

»edition psychosozial«

Vincentia Schroeter, Margit Koemeda-Lutz (Eds.)

# BIOENERGETIC ANALYSIS

The Clinical Journal of the International Institute
for Bioenergetic Analysis (2011) Volume 21

Psychosozial-Verlag

Bibliographic information of the Deutsche Nationalbibliothek
(The German Library)

The Deutsche Nationalbibliothek lists this publication in the
Deutsche Nationalbibliografie; detailed bibliographic data are available
in the Internet at http://dnb.d-nb.de.

Original edition
© 2011 Psychosozial-Verlag
E-mail: info@psychosozial-verlag.de
www.psychosozial-verlag.de
Cover: Ernst Ludwig Kirchner: »Pair of Acrobats, Sculpture«, 1932–33,
Oil on canvas, 85,5 x 72 cm
Draft design cover: Hanspeter Ludwig, Giessen
www.imaginary-art.net
ISBN 978-3-8379-2107-6

# Contents

Contents

## Creative Writing Section

**Reviewers for this issue were:**
*Mae Nascimento, Margit Koemeda-Lutz, Vincentia Schroeter,
Phil Helfaer, Linda Neal, Tarra Stariell, Helen Resneck-Sannes*

# Letter from the Editor

Dear Colleagues,

Welcome to the 21st volume of the clinical journal, Bioenergetic Analysis. One of the benefits of being a member of the IIBA is to receive this journal. A new volume is published annually. Clinical or research papers with relevance to the practice of Bioenergetic therapy are considered each summer. Papers must be submitted to the editor during the summer. Recently some IIBA conferences have been held in October. Papers presented as keynotes or presentations at these Bioenergetic conferences are not automatically considered for publication. An author who wants a paper to be considered must email their paper to the editor *between June and September*. The paper will be sent to at least two reviewers. The author's name is removed form the paper during review. The reviewers, therefore, do not know who wrote the paper. This aids in objectivity. A process of consideration ensues. Papers are accepted, rejected, or sent for revision.

The recent IIBA conference in Brazil was called, "The Poetry of the Body". Inspired by that theme, we have a new category in the journal this year. It is for creative writing. Creative pieces with content relating to the interests of therapists were considered. There are two sets of poetry in this volume. There are also three original papers. Bob Lewis writes passionately on the poetry of the body. His paper was adapted from his keynote in Brazil. James Allard writes a condensed version of his research on Bioenergetic therapy and the client's relationship with God. Jörg Clauer reports on fascinating new research on the *primary triad* in his paper considering aspects of grounding. These three authors are from three different countries, honoring our international flavor.

In the last volume we began a new process of translating the abstracts of the original papers into the five primary languages other than English, which are spoken by our members. These translations of abstracts will become a regular feature in the journal. The goal is to spark the interest of non-English reading members. If they are intrigued with the abstract, they are encouraged to translate the entire article for their local society. I want to thank the translators for this volume. Dankeschoen, Margit Koemeda. Le vous remercie, France Kauffman. Grazie, Rosaria Filoni. Obrigada, Camile Milagres. Gracias, Fina Pla.

The first person I ever heard about Bioenergetic Analysis from was Richard Mullins. He spoke in a graduate psychology class I was attending. I was instantly intrigued with his explanation of the body/mind duality and a form of working with chronic tension patterns in psychotherapy. He became one of my trainers when I attended Bioenergetic training in Northern California from 1976 to 1980. Dick Mullins died this past year. I asked my friend and colleague, Walt Watman, to write a memorial note for this volume. They were best friends. As a talented teacher, Dick was one of those people who affected and influenced generations who followed him into this work. To his family, his friends and to his Bioenergetic subgroup of colleagues who have maintained a support group since 1979, I offer my condolences for your loss. Dick Mullins was one of the strong threads that wove together the breathable fabric that has become our Bioenergetic community.

Our former chief editor, Margit Koemeda has completed a major work in writing a book about Bioenergetics and neuroscience, written for the lay public. Angela Klopstech reviews the book in this journal. Margit reviews a book about neuroscience by Joaquim Bauer. Currently, these books are only available in German. Bob Hilton reviews a book by Daniel Siegel. Both Dr. Siegel and Dr. Bauer will be keynote speakers at the upcoming IIBA conference to be held in San Diego, California, U.S.A., in October, 2011. Included in this volume is an invitation to this conference. It will be translated into six languages. We in San Diego are very excited to be hosting this major event. Besides Dr. Bauer, Daniel Siegel will also be an outside keynote speaker. We hope to welcome many of our international community members to our sunny shores next October.

Finally, I want to thank the authors for sending their original work published for your reading pleasure. I also want to thank the reviewers and editors who devoted their time and attention to the submissions we received this year. These editors and/or reviewers are Margit Koemeda, Mae Nasciemento, Phil Helfaer, Linda Neal, Helen Resneck-Sannes, Tarra Stariell, and Angela Klopstech.

I hope you enjoy this volume.

Warm Regards,

*Vincentia Schroeter*
Encinitas, California, USA
November 16, 2010

# Memorial Note

## Richard Mullins: July 1, 1940 – July 24, 2010

*Walt Watman*

He is gone, passed, dead. He was here, now he is not. We were friends for 42 years and Dick often said we were brothers with the same jewish mother, although he was a wasp from Kansas and I am jewish and from New York.

"Have courage brother, to stay with what is right for you", he once said to me and he lived by that, demonstrating for many others that they could as well. I am reminded of that valuable guidance often.

Although he was exceptionally intelligent and accomplished in the usual sense of having advanced degrees from high quality and well thought of schools, I never heard him mention or utilize the prestige they offered in order to announce himself or try to impress anyone. This was typical of him: quiet, deliberate, substantive, exceedingly competent, genuinely humble and unusually generous.

Anything he did was done well and he gave greatly of himself to bio-energetics, as a trainer, a clinical supervisor, and as part of the efforts at governance. Many people came to be better therapists as a result of his help and they in turn helped others.

He gave his heart, time, money, consistency, persistence, and clear thinking to many other organizations as well. I believe the rippling effect of that is one way Dick will continue to serve and be remembered.

I, fortunately, was considered a part of his family and, like his three children, Brian, Jeff and Kathryn, always felt welcomed, invited, encouraged and replenished when spending time with him at the family compound in Napa. Being with Dick there was always restorative for me and he made that possible matter of factly, lovingly, without fanfare. That made it easier to feel the gift of loving and being loved.

A fan of all things about trains, he would often visit railroad museums and take a ride on a train with no particular concern about where it might be going.

The last train has left the station Dick and, along with my freely flowing tears and great sadness, l feel the loneliness standing out here watching you, and it, disappear slowly, gently, into the distance ...

Goodbye my loved friend and brother, good bye ...

## ABOUT THE AUTHOR

Walt Watman, PhD
Clinical Psychologist
Certified Bioenergetic Therapist
Emeryville, CA. USA

# Introduction to Abstracts (in 6 languages)

*Vincentia Schroeter*

## Abstract Translations

A new feature in the IIBA Clinical Journal will be translations of the abstracts or summaries of the academic papers into five languages in addition to English. Below you will find abstracts of three original papers. We provide this service in consideration of those IIBA members who cannot read the articles in English. We hope to broaden the reading audience, and in so doing, honor the spirit of being a truly international community. We also hope the translated abstracts may lead groups to provide translation of the whole article for distribution.

## Übersetzung der Zusammenfassungen (German)

Neu ist in der Klinischen Zeitschrift des IIBA, dass die Zusammenfassungen der wissenschaftlichen Artikel neben Englisch in fünf weitere Sprachen übersetzt werden. Nachstehend finden Sie die Zusammenfassungen von drei Originalbeiträgen. Wir bieten diesen Dienst für IIBA-Mitglieder an, die die englischen Artikel nicht lesen können. Damit hoffen wir, unsere Leserschaft zu vergrößern und dem Geist einer wahrhaft internationalen Gemeinschaft zu dienen. Wir hoffen außerdem, dass die übersetzten Zusammenfassungen einzelne Gruppierungen dazu anregen wird, Übersetzungen ganzer Artikel zur weiteren Verteilung zu veranlassen.

*Translated by Margit Koemeda*

## TRADUCTIONS DE RESUME (FRENCH)

Une nouveauté dans le Journal Clinique de l'IIBA va être la traduction des résumés des articles académiques en cinq langues en plus de l'anglais. Vous trouverez ci-dessous les résumés de trois articles nouveaux. Nous offrons ce service sachant que certains de nos membres ne comprennent pas l'anglais. Nous espérons élargir le nombre de lecteurs, et cela faisant, honorer l'esprit d'une vraie communauté internationale. Nous espérons également que ces résumés traduits puissent amener les groupes à offrir la traduction de l'ensemble de l'article pour distribution.

*Translated by France Kauffmann*

## TRADUCCIONES DE RESÚMENES (SPANISH)

Una nueva característica de la Revista Clínica del IIBA será la traducción de los resúmenes de los artículos a cinco idiomas además del inglés. Debajo encontrareis los resúmenes de tres artículos.Ofrecemos este servicio en consideración a los miembros del IIBA que no pueden leer los artículos en inglés.Esperamos ampliar el público lector y al hacerlo honrar el espíritu de ser una verdadera comunidad internacional.Tambien albergamos la esperanza de que los resúmenes traducidos puedan propiciar que distintos grupos puedan proveer la traducción del artículo completo para su distribución.

*Translated by Fina Pla*

## TRADUZIONE DEGLI ABSTRACT (ITALIAN)

Un nuovo servizio della rivista dell'IIBA saranno le traduzioni degli abstract o dei riassunti dei saggi in cinque lingue oltre l'inglese. Di seguito troverete gli abstract di tre articoli originali. Forniamo questo servizio in considerazione del fatto che non tutti i soci dell'IIBA sono in grado di leggere gli articoli in inglese. Ci auguriamo di far crescere il numero dei lettori, e facendo ciò, onorare lo spirito di essere una vera comunità internazionale. Ci auguriamo anche che gli abstract tradotti possano stimolare alla traduzione e alla diffusione dell'intero articolo.

*Translated by Rosaria Filoni*


## TRADUÇÕES DE RESUMOS (PORTUGUESE)

Uma novidade que o periódico do IIBA irá oferecer será a publicação dos resumos e sumários de dissertações acadêmicas, agora traduzidos para cinco línguas, além do inglês. Abaixo vocês encontrarão resumos de três dissertações originais. Nós estamos provendo este serviço em consideração a aqueles membros do IIBA que não conseguem ler os artigos em inglês. Desejamos que desta forma o público leitor cresça, e desta forma, possamos honrar o espírito de ser uma verdadeira comunidade internacional. Também temos esperança de que os resumos traduzidos motivem alguns grupos a oferecerem traduções para o artigo completo, para que assim possamos fazer sua distribuição.

*Translated by Camile Milagres*

# Neurobiology and Psychological Development of Grounding and Embodiment

## Applications in the Treatment of Clients with Early Disorders[1]

*Jörg Clauer*

## Abstracts

### English

Alexander Lowen's concept of "grounding" is unique to Bioenergetic Analysis (BA). The bioenergetic grounding concept can scientifically be based on cerebral representations and integration of sensations – especially on proprioception allied with sense of equilibrium and touch. In addition, it is an operationalization of Freud's principle of reality, i. e., it is oriented to reality in the here and now. Bioenergetic techniques, stimulating the integration of "body-maps" like vestibular perception, proprioception and touch, may improve consciousness, vitality and cohesion of the self in various groups of clients with early disorders. Neurobiology, modern philosophy and system theory not only proclaim the end of the Cartesian duality of body and mind, but also demonstrate, how the perception and consciousness of our self is based on such body-maps.

In this paper the concept of grounding is mainly being conceived of

---

1 This paper is an updated version of an article first published in a German journal of psychoanalytic orientation (Clauer 2009). Part of this work was presented in Paris (November 2008 at the first international congress of body psychotherapy of ISC and EABP).

as relational and rooted in the psychosomatic self. Furthermore, a developmental perspective of grounding is elaborated, based on scientific findings on the primary triad of baby, mother and father. These results may gain importance as organizing principles in body-psychotherapy. Three case vignettes illustrate principles of grounding, cooperation and deconstruction from the perspective of client and therapist.

*Key words:* cooperation, deconstruction, embodied self, grounding, participation, triad

## NEUROBIOLOGIE UND DIE PSYCHISCHE ENTWICKLUNG VON GROUNDING UND EMBODIMENT (GERMAN)

Das Konzept des Grounding von Alexander Lowen ist einzigartig und steht für das Spezifische der Bioenergetischen Analyse (BA). Das Grounding-Konzept lässt sich wissenschaftlich mit den Repräsentationen und der Integration sensorischer Wahrnehmungen im Gehirn in Verbindung bringen – besonders mit der Tiefensensibilität (Proprioception) zusammen mit dem Gleichgewichtssinn und dem Berührungsempfinden. Zudem ist es eine Konkretisierung des Freudschen Realitätsprinzips, d. h. Grounding ist mit der Wahrnehmung der Realität im "Hier und Jetzt" verknüpft. Neurobiologie, moderne Philosophie und Systemtheorie proklamieren nicht nur den Abschied von der cartesianischen Leib-Seele-Spaltung; sie zeigen auch, wie unsere Selbst-Wahrnehmung und unser Bewusstsein in den Körperwahrnehmungen und den entsprechenden "Körperlandkarten" des Gehirns verwurzelt sind. Bioenergetische Methoden zur Verbesserung der Wahrnehmungen aus Gleichgewichtsorgan, Propriozeption und Berührung und der Integration der entsprechenden "Körperlandkarten" im Gehirn können die Bewusstheit, die Vitalität und Kohäsion des Selbst bei verschiedenen Gruppen von "Früh-Gestörten" Klienten fördern.

Dieser Beitrag betrachtet das Grounding-Konzept vornehmlich aus einer relational-interaktionellen Perspektive und als Ergebnis unseres verkörperten psychosomatischen Selbsterlebens. Außerdem wird eine entwicklungspsychologische Perspektive des Grounding vorgestellt, die auf Forschungen über die primäre Triade von Säugling, Mutter und Vater basiert. Die Ergebnisse könnten als organisierende Prinzipien in der Körperpsychotherapie unserer Patienten Bedeutung erlangen. Die Prinzipien und therapeutischen Möglichkeiten von Grounding, Kooperation und der Dekonstuktion der Perspektiven des Klienten und Therapeuten werden durch drei Fallbeispiele erläutert.

*Schlüsselwörter:* Beteiligung, Dekonstruktion, Grounding, Kooperation, verkörpertes Selbsterleben, Triade

## NOTES SUR LA NEUROBIOLOGIE ET LE DEVELOPPEMENT PSYCHOLOGIQUE DE L'ENRACINEMENT ET L'INCARNATION. APPLICATIONS DANS LE TRAITEMENT DES CLIENTS AYANT DES TROUBLES PRÉCOCES (FRENCH)

Le concept d' "enracinement" de Alexander Lowen est unique à l'Analyse Bioénergétique (BA). Le concept d'enracinement bioénergétique peut être basé scientifiquement sur les représentations cérébrales et l'intégration de sensations – spécialement sur la proprioception alliée à un sens de l'équilibre et du toucher et donc de l'enracinement neurobiologique de notre propre conscience au-dedans de notre self somatique et de nos relations interpersonnelles. De plus, c'est le principe de réalité de Freud rendu opérationnel c.à.d. qu'il est orienté vers la réalité dans l'ici et maintenant. Les techniques bioénergétiques, en stimulant l'intégration de "cartes du corps" comme la perception vestibulaire, la proprioception et le toucher, peuvent améliorer la conscience, la vitalité et la cohésion du self dans des groupes de clients variés ayant des troubles "précoces". La Neurobiologie, la philosophie moderne et la théorie systémique proclament non seulement la fin de la dualité du corps et de l'esprit Cartésienne, mais démontrent aussi, comment la perception et la conscience de notre self sont basées sur de telles cartes du corps.

Dans cet article le concept d'enracinement est principalement conçu comme relationnel et enraciné dans le self psychosomatique. De plus, une perspective de l'enracinement selon le développement est élaborée, basée sur les découvertes scientifiques de la triade primaire bébé, mère

19

et père. Ces résultats peuvent gagner en importance en tant que principes organisateurs en psychothérapie corporelle. Trois vignettes de cas illustrent les principes d'enracinement, coopération et déconstruction à partir de la perspective du client de du thérapeute.

*Mots Clé:* coopération, déconstruction, self incarné, enracinement, participation, triade

## APUNTES SOBRE NEUROBIOLOGÍA Y DESARROLLO PSICOLÓGICO DEL GROUNDING Y LA CORPOREIDAD. APLICACIONES EN EL TRATAMIENTO DE CLIENTES CON TRASTORNOS PREMATUROS (SPANISH)

El concepto de "grounding", de Alexander Lowen es específico del Análisis Bioenergético (AB). El concepto bioenergético de enraizamiento puede basarse científicamente en las representaciones cerebrales y en la integración de sensaciones – especialmente en la propiocepción junto con un sentido del equilibrio y del contacto y entonces el enraizamiento neurobiológico de nuestra auto-percepción desde nuestro self somático y desde las relaciones interpersonales. Además, es un funcionamiento del principio de realidad de Freud, por ejemplo, está orientado a la realidad en el aquí y ahora.

Las técnicas bioenergéticas, estimulando la integración de "mapas corporales" como la percepción vestibular, la propiocepción y el contacto, pueden mejorar la conciencia, vitalidad y cohesión del self en varios grupos de clientes con "desórdenes tempranos". La neurobiología, la filosofía moderna y la teoría sistémica no solo proclaman el fin de la dualidad Cartesiana de cuerpo y mente, sino que también demuestran cómo la percepción y conciencia del self se basa en tales "mapas corporales".

En este artículo el concepto de grounding es fundamentalmente concebido como relacional y enraizado en el self psicosomático. Además, una perspectiva evolutiva del grounding es elaborada, basada en los conocimientos científicos acerca de la tríada bebé, madre y padre. Estos resultados pueden ganar importancia como principios organizadores en la psicoterapia corporal. Las viñetas de tres casos ilustran los principios de grounding, cooperación y deconstrucción desde la perspectiva de cliente y terapeuta.

*Palabras clave:* Cooperación, deconstrucción, self corpóreo, enraizamiento, participación, tríada.

## NOTE SULLA NEUROBIOLOGIA E SULLO SVILUPPO PSICOLOGICO DEL GROUNDING E DELL'EMBODIMENT. APPLICAZIONE NEL TRATTAMENTO DI PAZIENTI CON DISTURBI PRECOCI (ITALIAN)

Il concetto di grounding di A. Lowen è originale dell'analisi bioenergetica. Da un punto di vista scientifico si basa sulle rappresentazioni cerebrali e sull'integrazione delle sensazioni – specialmente sulla propriocezione, connessa al senso di equilibrio e al contatto, e quindi come radicamento neurobiologico dell'auto-consapevolezza nel Sé somatico e nella relazionalità. Inoltre, è un modo di rendere operativo il concetto di "principio di realtà" di Freud, per esempio è orientato alla realtà dell' hic et nunc. Le tecniche bioenergetiche, che stimolano l'integrazione delle "mappe corporee" quali la percezione vestibolare, la propriocezione e il contatto, possono arricchire la consapevolezza, la vitalità e la coesione del Sé in vari gruppi di pazienti che soffrono di disturbi precoci. La neurobiologia, la filosofia moderna e la teoria dei sistemi non solo proclamano la fine del dualismo cartesiano di corpo e mente, ma dimostrano anche che la percezione e la consapevolezza del nostro Sé si basa su tali mappe corporee.

In questo saggio il concetto di grounding è concepito come relazionale e radicato nel Sé psicosomatico. Inoltre, viene elaborata una prospettiva evolutiva del grounding, basata su scoperte scientifiche che riguardano la triade primaria di bambino, madre e padre. Questi risultati possono risultare importanti come principi organizzatori della psicoterapia corporea. Tre vignette cliniche illustrano i concetti di grounding, cooperazione e decostruzione dal punto di vista del paziente e del terapeuta.

*Parole chiave:* Cooperazione, decostruzione, Sé incarnato, grounding, partecipazione, triade

## NOTAS SOBRE NEUROBIOLOGIA E DESENVOLVIMENTO PSICOLÓGICO DO ENRAIZAMENTO(GROUNDING) E DA CORPORIFICAÇÃO. APLICAÇÕES NO TRATAMENTO DE CLIENTES COM TRANSTORNOS PRECOCES (PORTUGUESE)

O conceito de "grounding" vindo de Alexander Lowen é exclusivo da Análise Bioenergética (AB). Este conceito – grounding bioenergético – pode ser cientificamente baseado nas representações cerebrais e integração de sensações – especialmente em propriocepção aliada com o senso de equilíbrio e de toque e, portanto, o enraizamento neurobiológico da nossa auto-consciência dentro de nosso self somático e dentro de relacionamentos interpessoais. Além disso, é uma operacionalização do princípio Freudiano de realidade, ou seja, é orientado à realidade no aqui e agora. As técnincas Bioenergéticas, estimuladoras da integração dos "mapas corporais" como percepção vestibular, propriocepção e o toque, podem aprimorar a consciência, a vitalidade e a coesão do self em vários grupos de clientes com transtornos precoces. A Neurobiologia, a filosofia moderna e a teoria de sistemas não apenas proclamam o fim da dualidade cartesiana entre o corpo e a mente, mas também demonstram como a percepção e a consciência de nosso self é baseado em tais mapas do corpo.

Neste artigo o conceito de *grounding* está principalmente sendo concebido como sendo relacional e enraizado no self psicossomático. Além disso, uma perspectiva de desenvolvimento de grounding é elaborado com base em conclusões científicas sobre a tríade primária: bebê, mãe e pai. Estes resultados podem ganhar importância como organizadores dos princípios da psicoterapia corporal. Três casos irão ilustrar os princípios do *grounding*, cooperação e desconstrução a partir da perspectiva do cliente e do terapeuta.

*Palavras chave:* cooperação, desconstrução, self corporificado, grounding, participação, tríade

## INTRODUCTION

One of the most significant contributions of the recently deceased founder of Bioenergetic Analysis, Alexander Lowen, is his concept of grounding. Bioenergetic therapists understand it as rootedness in the reality of ones own body, of ones own history, in relationships and in the reality of a person as lived here and now. "Grounding stands for the uniqueness of Bioenergetic Analysis that can not be confused with other theoretical and practical orientations of psychotherapy. The concept of grounding does not exist in psychoanalytic literature and emerged when Alexander Lowen ... began to work with breathing and the body in the standing position ... The psychoanalyst was brought out of his passive-abstinent role ... Grounding was intended to reconnect the patient with the ground of reality." (Oelmann 1996, p. 129 (translation by author, which hereafter will be referred to as tba.)). Lowen has developed grounding as a new corner pillar of his energetic perspective. The charging in the upper half of our body and the longitudinal or pendular swing of our energetic charge needs discharge through the lower half of the body downward into the earth or as sexual discharge (Lowen 1958, p. 78ff.+92, Helfaer 1998, p. 65ff.). "We move by discharge of energy into the ground ... All energy finds its way eventually into the earth; this is the principle known as "grounding." It explains the discharge through storm and lightening of the overcharged atmosphere. This principle must also underlie the sexual act" (Lowen 1958, p. 80).

In bioenergetic therapy grounding can be seen as an important acquisition to prevent experiences of dissolution of boundaries, dissociation and loss of reality. It is also a concretization of Freud's reality principle: "Being grounded means being in touch with reality" (Lowen 1978, p. 48). "The difference (to Freud, author's note) is, that it is not restricted to cognitive understanding" (Pechtl 1980, p. 193, translation by author (tba.)). Also grounding circumscribes the holding a person receives through the voice, eye contact, touch, and physical contact in relation with another person. In this paper the concept of grounding is mainly being conceived of as relational and rooted in the embodied self.

The concept of grounding is mostly associated with six realms:
a)     Upright gait in the gravity field of the earth – i. e. the contact with

23

the ground, secure stance and autonomy, which we do not have in the early days of our life as a baby;
b) Feeling contact with all realms of ones own physicality – i.e. the rootedness in the perception and awareness of the bodily-self (i.e. the phenomenal self model);
c) As a precondition for containment (emotional holding capacity) and discharge of excitement into the ground;
d) The ability to connect and maintain relationships, to love;
e) The ability to tolerate the dissolution of boundaries of self or dissociation in the sense of connectedness with a higher power or spiritual dimension (transcendence);
f) Connectedness with ones own history, understanding of ones biography;

As Bioenergetic therapists we expect that the importance of embodiment and grounding in particular will be reflected in findings of neurobiology. Nonetheless, it is relieving to really find these scientific roots in neurobiology, systems theory and modern philosophy. This can be helpful to explain our knowledge to the modern world that believes in scientific proof. Lowe, like Freud, was eagerly looking for biological explanations and he connected his concept of grounding to the phylogenetic development of the human species (c. Lowen 1958, p. 70ff.). Our unique development has been inseparably linked with the evolution of the *upright gait* and thus our hands became free for using tools. Learning by imitation and playful acquisition of skills in the group then represented an essential advantage for survival. The precondition of a development viewed in this way is a tremendous achievement of integration of the signals. These signals come from the organ of equilibrium (vestibular system) as well as touch and perception of position in space/ depth sensitivity (proprioception). All these systems of the body developed in the brain so that upright walking became possible. This is one of the many explanations for the eminent significance of grounding. The neurobiological implications of this subject and their applications in therapy will be the *first part* of this article.

*Cooperation* in hunting or gathering bands led to a further developmental leap. For this reason refining of the exchange of signals became increasingly important, and that encouraged affect attunement by facial expression and collaboration by gestures as well as the development of language[2]. Recently, in the discovery of one of our ancestors, "Ardipithecus ramidus" researchers discuss that the *cooperation* of the parents in bringing up the infants was an important step in human evolution (Lovejoy 2009). The upright gait and thus new form of grounding as a unique characteristic of our human species is not to be found in early childhood. The baby needs to be grounded in the relationship to his/her caregivers and its excitement and affects need their help to be regulated, either to be calmed (discharged) or to be stimulated/vitalized. Lowen (1958, p. 108+56) points to this: "... and reality for the child is its mother." It is fascinating that the research of the primary triangle of mother, baby *and* father shows that contact and mutual affect regulation needs is based on the orientation and organization of the lower half of the body that according to Lowen (1958) is closely connected to grounding. The *second part* of this paper involves the developments and therapeutic implications of this triad research. In the developing infant the intense struggle for his own upright gait, grounding and consciousness can be observed easily. The developmental steps of phylogenesis are thus reproduced in ontogenesis.

The development of our embodied self, our selfhood, in the first years of our lives can be subject to limitations, disturbances or traumatic events (Stern 1985, Schore 1992). The outcome of such events we will find in our clients with "early" disorders. Three case examples are included in this paper to illustrate the value and therapeutic use of the principles and knowledge described here. Like in childhood our therapeutic affect attunement and collaboration is not and should not be perfect. Miscoordinations or interruptions in affect attunement or collaboration always need to happen. The important step for the development of the baby and our patients as well is the reestablishment/reconstruction of attunement and collaboration in the relationship. Within the therapy process this reconstruction of the collaboration and affect attunement is fostered or enabled by a process of "*deconstruction*" of the perspective of patient and therapist. This is the subject of the *third case vignette* of this article.

---

2  A further development of my ideas concerning this subject you will find in: Forum der Bioenergetischen Analyse 2011.

## PART 1: NEUROBIOLOGICAL ASPECTS
## OF EMBODIMENT AND GROUNDING

In Bioenergetic therapy grounding can be seen as an important acquisition to prevent experiences of dissolution of boundaries, dissociation and loss of reality. The developmental model of Bioenergetic Analysis expanded by the results of infant, attachment and neurobiological research offers an understanding of therapeutic relationship and processes, which provides a safe frame and developmental space for patients suffering from personality disorders. It led to an emphasis of a safe therapeutic working relationship as well as differentiated approaches of treatment for individuals with different life experiences and types of disorders (Heinrich-Clauer 2008). Also, grounding circumscribes the holding a person receives through the voice, eye contact, touch, and physical contact in relation with another person too. Rootedness, i. e. the building of a secure self-structure with the perception of their own body and the therapeutic relationship is particularly important for patients suffering from disruptions of the coherence of self. "Relationship has a grounding effect for the therapeutic process […]. This view does not contradict Lowen's notion that grounding can be achieved mainly through the energy flow in legs and feet and the contact with the ground of an individual. But it is not just a question of grounding techniques, whether clients in the therapeutic situation are able to be really grounded or not … In order to be able to integrate the doubtlessly stabilizing and vitalizing experience of the energy flow in legs and feet and the good feeling of ones own stance in the therapeutic situation into ones sense of self, a relational response of the present therapist is essential. Clients need to be able to relate to themselves and to the other while perceiving body sensations and trying to communicate them verbally. *Relatedness of the therapist* means mindful looking, sensing and listening as well as the ability to verbally confirm and propose words for the integration of the experience" (Heinrich 2001, p. 68 (tba.)).

The first case vignette elucidates the importance of the inclusion of resonance (Heinrich-Clauer 1997 and 2008), grounding and exploration of one's own body in a critical situation to foster integration processes.

## CASE VIGNETTE 1: A HALLUCINATORY EPISODE

A 55-year-old female teacher suffering from sleep disturbance, alcohol dependency, severe depression, dependent-narcissistic personality traits and living in a traumatizing relationship was in inpatient treatment. In addition to verbal psychodynamic individual therapy with me, she worked with concentrative movement therapy (CMT) in a group setting. After a couple of weeks she appeared to be stabilized and abstinent from addictive substances. One Friday afternoon I received a phone call from the CMT colleague. With an excited voice she described her distress with the patient. Later on, when I was alone with the patient in my office, I understood my colleague being so upset. In front of me I saw a sweating, highly restless, fearful patient. After a while, in spite of my own tightness, I managed to find out what she experienced bodily and mentally. She felt helplessly and physically exposed, because she saw the big erect genital of a man on the wall. (I suppose she suffered from an alcoholic hallucinosis. Background for the form of the hallucination was that she was daily forced by her husband to have intercourse with him.) For a while I felt downright uncomfortable in this emotionally charged atmosphere and shared her helplessness. Then I noticed how in my standing position I involuntarily worked (like in Bioenergetic exercise groups) into my legs and ankle joints in moving with slightly bent knees gently back and forth in my feet and ankle joints. [I was looking for a secure stance and in this way dealt with my feelings of insecurity and helplessness.] I invited the patient to try something similar as I did and also to stamp lightly with her feet on the ground. When she hereupon had somewhat quieted down, I asked her to describe the apparition on the wall more precisely. In touching the wall with my hand I managed to encourage her to explore the wall at the place of the apparition together with me. In this process she became quieter and the hallucination disappeared. After this her therapy made significant progress, as the work on her conflicts and traumatization was enhanced by this episode.

Conclusion: Instead of exploring the obvious fear and transferential situation (which would have needed more contact with reality from the patient) I relied on my experience as a bioenergetic therapist and helped my patient and myself in this critical situation with grounding and contact with reality. In the therapy situation I shared the feelings and excitement of the patient implicitly in my embodied countertransference (resonance) and carried (contained) them with her. The perception of my resonance opened for me a way to direct the attention of the patient to her body, her contact with the ground and then to re-establish contact with reality together with her. Beside containment/grounding of the therapist, the patient's *contact with the ground* and the mutual *tactile exploration* and the *touch* itself were important elements of the therapy process. "Bringing one's self back to a sense of the feet on the ground allows one to bring oneself back to an ongoing sense of self-regulation and self-respect." (Helfaer 1998, p. 70).

## GROUNDING IN THE THERAPEUTIC RELATIONSHIP

Grounding, either in the standing position or by sitting in front of each other, enhances the orientation to the reality principle, adult functioning, (i.e. the integrative ego-functions) and guides patients in their exploration. Settings based on the lying position can have a regressive function. When the relational context and experiential background of the patient are disregarded they can lead to dissociative phenomena, depersonalization and ultimately psychotic decompensation. Reinert (2007, p. 504f.) a psychoanalyst, describes such cases and takes them as a cause to caution against: "Dangers of the inclusion of the body in therapy: More severely disturbed Borderline patients with insecure ego-boundaries would be massively overstrained by such an immediate confrontation with their physical experience." He describes a patient, "with a Borderline structure with severe secondary addictive disorder ..." (Ibid.). In his first therapy session already in the lying position without an instruction that would have provided a framing by the therapist, the patient got into severe dissociation and states of excitement. As a bioenergetic analyst one misses here the application of therapeutic (grounding) principles providing for structure and holding and a discussion of the effect of the relational context. Without working on contact with the ground (reality principle) and without exploration and clarifying of the relationship with his own body as well as with the therapist, a lying setting for such patients is hardly imaginable for a Bioenergetic analyst. The significance of physical interaction and grounding in the therapy process of a bor-derline patient will later be the subject of the second case vignette.

The very experience with events of dissolution of boundaries has led to a further development of Bioenergetic Analysis. Especially important is the integration of impulses from the face musculature (emotional perception) with those of body movements (ibid. p. 44). Body move-ments, our expectation of movements and intentions are mainly directed by the integration of information from depth sensitivity (proprioception), sense of equilibrium and touch (Blakeslee & Blakeslee, hereafter referred to as B&B p. 29). According to the Bioenergetic concept of "cephalic shock" (Lewis 2008), the integration of this information can be disturbed by a layer of tension at the base of the skull and in the region of the eyes (Lowen 1978, p. 58). These tensions lead to disinte-gration or lack of integration of information coming from the organ of equilibrium, visual perceptions and depth sensitivity. Lewis related his concept to Winnicott's concept of the "false self". He described the physical side of dissociation, which according to Schore (2002), is an outcome of trauma-induced developmental disturbances. Seen from the perspective of developmental psychology, the infant lacks the holding of body and soul, which is the foundation for the development of a cohesive self. According to Bioenergetic experiential knowledge, the integration of body perception can be seen as surrounding the center of the diaphragm/Hara/like an onion. From the perspective of the functional unity of body and soul, the area at the base of skull and around the eyes functionally corresponds with ankle joints and feet. Sense of equilibrium, secure stance and the ability to let oneself down into the ground are as disturbed as the ability to surrender to a partner in a relationship.

## THE TRUE SELF AND OUR CONSCIOUS MIND IS ROOTED IN PROPRIOCEPTION

*The central anchor of our true self in the body is the proprioceptive sen-sations.* Winnicott (1974, p. 193f.) was engaged in this subject: "The true self comes from aliveness of body tissue and the agency of body functions including the functioning of heart and breathing ... The true self emerges as soon as there is some psychological organization of the individual, and it means little more than the totality of sensomotor aliveness." "Whenever conscious experience occurs (i.e. activation of a stable integrated model of reality [in the brain, author's note]), also this continuous source of inner, proprioceptive input exists" (Metzinger 2005, p. 19; hereafter quoted as Met. (tba.)). Damasio (2000) refers to this as *core self*, (a term used by Stern [1985] for the development of the infant) that is dependent on the constant neuronal activity of those brain regions of the body self, which are independent from external input (that means independent from sensations like seeing and hearing). In bioenergetic therapy we experience this fact in patients with diminished grounding and fear of falling. They try to compensate the insecurity within their self and their contact to reality by controlling the world by visual information. If they close their eyes they may lose their sense of equilibrium, feel very insecure and may get in a panic.

## 1.1.  EMBODIMENT AND GROUNDING FOSTER
### THE COHESION AND VITALITY OF THE SELF

Our self-perception (and introspection) is not a passive reception process but an active construction procedure (B&B, p. 41). Disturbances of body perception or integration of body maps in the brain leads to disturbances of the cohesion of the self. These have been investigated thoroughly by self-psychology. Early traumatization of the infant (by violence, abuse or neglect) instead of developing a vital and cohesive (integrated) self (-model) leads to depressive-depleted/devitalized or *fragmented/dissociated* self states (e.g. Lichtenberg 2000, Schore 2002). Depleted/devitalized self-states we find in depressions that are frequently connected with a sense of emptiness and missing holding, a silent void or black hole of nothingness, a groundlessness (Clauer 2007, Schore 2002). The importance of the stimulation of body perception and grounding in the case of depression is part of our common knowledge in body psychotherapy (e.g. Lowen 1972, Clauer & Koemeda-Lutz 2010).

During growth spurts of children and adolescents there frequently occurs a temporary disturbance of proprioceptive perception of the body and a sense as if they have lost their feet or legs (B&B, p. 29). Difficulties in adolescents of orientation in reality that correspond with this loss of grounding are well known. Their urge for motor activity might have a self-healing effect in this process. Like in a young mammal, feedback from its own bodily movements provides meaning to what it experiences.

There is a similar state of "hovering above ground" associated with restriction of contact with reality in depressions and psychoses. As a psychiatrist I have experienced a number of floridly paranoid-hallucinatory patients, who "hovered above ground" on their toes during a phase of deep fear. B&B have described how the impairments of depth sensitivity and sense of equilibrium can lead to illusionary misperceptions.

Proprioception is the predominantly unconscious perception of position and movement of our muscles, bones, joints, sinews and skin. "An especially large number of such sensors is situated in the facial skin, the *soles of the feet* and in the fingertips" (Storch, hereafter quoted as Sto., p. 96). The integration of depth sensitivity, sense of equilibrium and touch therefore can very well be enhanced by *stimulating the soles of the feet in various ways* as well as by dynamic grounding (Steckel 2006), and can be enhanced by Do-In exercises[3] (Clauer 2007). "Flummies" (small hard rubber balls of 2.5 (to 3.5) cm of diameter, i. e. one to one and a half inch of diameter) have been found to be very effective tools for stimulating the sole of a foot by stepping with one foot on the ball and slowly rolling back and forth (Vita Heinrich-Clauer, personal communication).

COHERENCE OF SELF IS ENABLED BY INTEGRATION OF "BODY MAPS"

Neurobiology and philosophy arrive at the same conclusion, that rootedness in the bodily self and especially in proprioception represents the foundation for ever more complex levels of consciousness. *Proprioception – integrated with sense of equilibrium, touch and somatovis-*

3 "Do-In" is a collection (set) of exercises (practices) and teachings about physical and mental development of the human being (Kushi 1994). I refer here to the part of "General practices", changed and supplemented by us. These exercises are a form of self-massage, which mobilizes especially the body surface, joints and musculoskeletal system.

*ceral sensations – is a central indispensable component of grounding and rootedness in the bodily self.* "The "balancing disk", also known as the "wobble board" can be an important tool in Bioenergetic analysis to foster the integration of these body senses, especially proprioception and sense of equilibrium. It has been applied independently by V. Heinrich-Clauer, K. Oelmann (personal communication), Clauer (2007) and Ehrensperger (2006) with many types of disorders. Alternatively the "airex balance pad" may be used (personal communication, H. Steckel). The neural integration of the different internal information of our body (self-awareness) in our brain seems to be a crucial process and step. Putting some pieces of the puzzle together might give us an important impulse for Bioenergetic therapy. In the treatment of diseases with disorders of body schema and body image for instance (psycho-) analysis of affect attunement, transference and countertransference *alone* are insufficient. "To bring the clients bodies and minds back together – to fire up their body schemas […] you need to try something more direct, more dynamic, more tactile, more proprioceptive. […] The wobble board provides a powerful entry into body schema repair via stimulation of the vestibular cortex. By putting balance at the center of attention, your body schema cannot be ignored" (B&B, p. 45f. cf. Bauer 2002, p. 190).

"Basically there are four types of internally generated information, which create a persisting functional link between the phenomenal self model and its physical base in the brain" (Met. p. 19 (tba.)): input from the *vestibular system* (sense of equilibrium); input from invariant parts of the *body image* (mainly *proprioception, touch,* temperature, pain); *somatovisceral* information from the intestines and the cardiovascular system; and input from brainstem and hypothalamus (that provides background emotions and moods, anchored in the biochemical landscape in the blood). B&B refer to the particular representation of the information in different neural networks of the brain as *"body maps"*: "The sum total of your numerous, flexible, morphable body maps gives rise to the solid-feeling subjective sense of "me-ness" and to your ability to comprehend and navigate the world around you. You can think of the maps as a mandala whose overall pattern creates your embodied, feeling self" (B&B, p. 12). An integrative system in the parietal brain seems to be part of the formation of the mandala, i. e. a representation of the system as a whole (B&B,

p. 51). The process of 'sensory integration' is an important long lasting process in childhood development up to the age of seven years and can be disturbed by many different reasons (Ayres 2002). The final classification and stable self-model seems to be a construct of the frontal brain. It needs circuits in a network between parietal brain and an analytic region in the frontal brain (Heinen 2010). The *embodied sense of self* corresponds to the existence of a *single, coherent and temporally stable self (model)* that is known as *selfhood*[4] i.e. prereflexive familiarity with oneself (Met. p. 8, 17, (tba.). This means nothing less than the functional centering of the phenomenal space (of the experiential irreducible ego sense) through physical anchoring. *When this physical anchoring is lost, the coherence of the self is also lost* with the consequence of denials, dissociations or ego disturbances like e.g. psychoses (ibid. p. 16f.). The formation of (higher) neural patterns (of the self-model) has to be embedded in body perception, otherwise hallucinations predominate. Concerning dissociative identity disturbances, the integrating system uses different and alternating self-models and the integration (e.g. of the optical and proprioceptive map) occurs not at all or in a distorted way (Metzinger 2005, p. 17f.). In the context of dissociative disorders, grounding has proved of value also in trauma psychotherapy (Bercelli 2005, Clauer 2007) to discharge the "frozen residue of energy" and enhancing body awareness and self-possession. The recalibration of body maps is a key to healing trauma (B&B; p. 48).

## 1.2. DISORDERS OF BODY SCHEMA AND BODY IMAGE: TOUCH AND CONTACT

Another form of the missing integration of the "body-maps" is to be found in eating disorders and (body-) dysmorphic disorders (e.g. dysmorphophobia), where the body scheme, the *integration of touch with depth sensitivity (proprioception) and sense of equilibrium* is changed (B&B, p. 51f.). Individuals with binge eating feel dissociated, as if body and brain inhabit mutually exclusive worlds." (B&B, p. 45). Modalities

---

4 Speaking of selfhood, Lowen (1984, S. 111) says it is comprised of self-awareness (self-perception), self-expression and self-possession.

that use body sensations as a key to healing (like Bioenergetic analysis and other physical therapies) enhance awareness and attentiveness, they recalibrate your body maps (your body schema awareness, which is mostly implicit) so that you can feel yourself from inside out and self-possession is enhanced (B&B, p. 37+48).

Beside the improvement of self-awareness, Bioenergetic psychotherapy also will address the more conscious body image and the shame affect and the system of self hate (Helfaer 2007, p. 63+67). The feeling, "who I am is shameful and that my body, body parts, and bodily expressions are shameful" will prevent self-respect and trust in being touched. The "body image" is a concept for our emotional response to how we experience our body, including how we dress, pose, move, and *believe others see us*. It is embedded both in our body maps and in the parts of our cortex that store our autobiographical memories and social attitudes and so can be drenched in shame (B&B, p. 42f.). Especially important in this respect is the integration of impulses from the face musculature (emotional perception) with those of body movements (ibid. p. 44).

Anorexia patients hate to be touched and they leave situations in which they are expected to have body contact with others. Research further suggests that they are suffering from such a mismatch between body maps of touch and vision, that their body schemas are unreliable (B&B, p. 50f.). In an experiment, a full-body neoprene suit an anorexic patient wore stimulated the tactile perception. "Before she wore the suit, when she was starving, her left hemisphere was dominant. After she wore the suit – and had gained several pounds – brain activity shifted to her right hemisphere, particularly to the parietal lobe" (B&B, p. 52). The integration of the brain maps in the right parietal lobe seemed to be restored.

We might connect this to the work of Schore (2002): "Traumatic attachment experiences negatively affect the early organization of the right brain," (p. 462). "Schore further stresses that the right hemisphere is centrally involved in the analysis of direct information from our own body … due to the fact that it contains more than the left extensive reciprocal connections with the autonomic nervous system (ANS) … The energy-expending sympathetic and energy-conserving parasympathetic circuits of the ANS generate the involuntary bodily functions that represent the somatic components of all emotional states (p. 445).

Mutual pleasant touch (especially on the front side of the torso) contact and sexuality with another being stimulates the parasympathetic system and raises the oxytocin level. Oxytocin is the hormone of calm and connection, of healing and growth. Touch not only creates an emotional bonding but also transmits the positive health and anti-stress effects of oxytocin (Uvnäs Moberg 2003, p. 89+127). "Touch is beneficial for human growth and health" (Ibid p. 111). So this might be an important effect in anorexics – that touch enhances parasympathetic inner responsiveness with the oxytocin balance and counteracts in this way the fight-flight-mechanism (and traumatization).

Touch and contact proves to be important for the healing of at least some patients with early disturbances like anorexia nervosa. The same (combined with balance and viscerosensitivity) I found to be the case for a patient with Colitis ulcerosa (Clauer 2007) where it was important too that: "Vestibular signals are intimately tied to touch … Nothing stabilizes balance better than light touches and contact with the environment."(B&B, p. 30f.). The integration of body maps of viscerosensitivity and of the brainstem will be fostered when we are working with breathing and other body rhythms (e. g. Buti-Zaccagnini 2008).

## 1.3.    BODY PERCEPTION (PROPRIOCEPTION, TOUCH AND SENSE OF EQUILIBRIUM) AND ITS INTEGRATION AS THE FOUNDATION FOR CONSCIOUSNESS AND COHERENCE OF THE SELF

Like grounding, *selfhood* is an important concept of Lowen's (1983, p. 111f.): "The goal (of bioenergetic analysis) may be described as the attainment of selfhood, which is comprised of self-awareness, self-expression and self-possession. Being aware of oneself means being fully in touch with the body, but that is possible only if the person gains insight into the unconscious motivations of behavior. Self expression denotes the ability to sense and express all feelings, while self possession means that one is in conscious command of this expression." Neurobiology, systems theory and the philosophy of the "self model" have also demonstrated the inseparable unity of psychological and physical experience and the rootedness of the self in the body.

From the viewpoint of systems theory we are self-organizing systems, whose conscious, increasingly complex, processing abilities rest on (recognizable) formation of neural patterns. Keeping Lowen (1978, p. 55) in mind: "Grounding roots a person in his animal or physical basic functions and in this way nourishes and supports his mental striving", we recognize that today's systems theory comes to a similar conclusion: that non-verbal, unconscious processes based on mental self-organization driven and shaped by feelings, body sensation and situation form the foundation of *intelligence*. (Storch et al. 2006, p. 34, (tba.)). Intelligent cognition (thinking as formation of neural patterns of a higher order) is unthinkable without it being embedded or rooted in body perception *and* without perception of the environment. (Sto., p. 30f.).

Neurobiological research even transcends this view and arrives at the conclusion that perceptions (of environment) make no sense except in the reference system of our embodied self: "As a young mammal in its formative stages moves around, feedback from its own bodily move-ments provides meaning to what it sees [...] If an animal is exposed to high-quality visual information but only as a passive observer, its brain will never learn what any of that visual information is supposed to mean. [...] The same goes for all the "special" senses: The body mandala is their central integrator, the mind's ultimate frame of reference, the underly-ing metric system of perception. Sensation doesn't make sense except in reference to your embodied self. [...] In contrast, vision or hearing without a body to relate sights and sounds to would be nothing but psychically empty patterns of information. Meaning is rooted in agency (the ability to act and choose), and agency depends on embodiment. [...] *Nothing truly intelligent is going to develop in a bodiless mainframe. In real life there is no such thing as a disembodied consciousness.*" (B&B, p. 11f.). This point of view was supported by research concerning artificial intelligence: "While we can readily use disembodied computers to ma-nipulate symbolic information, intelligence requires interaction with the world. In this view embodied cognition ... emphasizes what is enabled cognitively by having a body. Ironically, this knowledge turns out to be exceedingly difficult for robots to acquire ... embodied cognition leads to gains of cognitive function. There is growing evidence from studies in athletes that physical experience can improve perceptual ability" (Grafton (2009, p. 98).

A central subject of the "philosophy of a self-model" and of consciousness of Metzinger (2005, 2009) is his so called "phenomenal transparency", that I conceive of as a necessary fact: Not to know that our subjective feeling of me-ness or selfhood is only an neurological construct of our brain and to experience our self in direct and immediate (online) contact with oneself and the world is an important and necessary precondition, so that we are able to function in the world and enjoy it! "Phenomenal transparency" (ibid. p. 21f.) means that we are experientially not able to recognize the "self-model" created in the brain as such; instead of we experience ourselves as if we were in direct and immediate epistemic contact with ourselves.

Metzinger further elaborates: "From a transparent model of the system, a self emerges that is embedded in this reality [...] a dynamic phenomenal *online* (author's choice of word) simulation of the self as a subject integrated in the world by constantly changing relations through knowing and acting" (ibid. p. 25). "Malleable and ever more complex self models allow, not only an ongoing optimization of somatomotor, perceptual and cognitive functions, but later on also social cognitions and thereby the development of <u>*cooperative behavior*</u> (emphasis by the author). With them emerged the fundamental representational resources for adoption of perspectives, empathy and guilt, later on also for meta-cognitive accomplishments e.g. the development of a self-concept and a *theory of mind* (ibid. p. 11).


## PART 2: THE TRIAD RESEARCH: COOPERATION IN CHILD DEVELOPMENT AND BODY PSYCHOTHERAPY


### 2.1. FROM DYAD TO TRIAD AND COLLABORATION

During the last few decades, infant and attachment research have changed our psychotherapeutic work. Developmental research was mostly concerned with the dyadic relationship and the significance of our emotional attunement. For access to awareness and consciousness, psychoanalytic authors underline the experience of affect attunement, of attachment and intersubjectivity as privileged compared to interaction (e.g. Lichtenberg et al. 2000, p. 124). Research on the family triad, i.e. the interaction of infant, mother *and* father represents a connective link and has emphasized the significance of the *cooperative interaction* (Fivaz-Depeursinge & Corboz-Warnery 2001, hereafter quoted as F&C). The physical organizing principles of cooperation in the triad described in this research fascinated me, since I recognized their value in my therapeutic work with adult patients. The ability for cooperation is among the highest developed cohesive self-functions of the human being (Met, p. 11). Downing (2007, p. 558f.) referred to cooperative interaction as "collaborative connection" (i.e. mutual coordination for the accomplishment of a practical goal). He highlights it as an important independent category of intersubjectivity: "If it is correct, that the ability for cooperation follows its own separate strands of development, then its inclusion (in therapy, author's note) is virtually called for" (Downing 2007, p. 561).

At least for the development of the child and the family alliances, "cooperation, liveliness and grace prevail over adversity" (F&C, p. 9). After finishing this paper this perspective was supported by the recent scientific discovery of one of our ancestors "Ardipithecus ramidus". There is a discussion that the male for the first time in phylogeny became a partner in the *cooperation* of the parents in bringing up the infants. The new perspective is that this could have been an important and possibly crucial step in human evolution (Lovejoy 2009).

## 2.2. THE "LAUSANNE-TRILOGUE-PLAY"

In their "Lausanne-Trilogue-Play" F&C have investigated play scenes of infant, mother *and* father (known as the triad) during the child's first year of life in a standardized frame using video recordings. The defined and specified task consisted of four determined segments of play. First, one parent was supposed to play with the infant, then the other parent and then the three of them together, and finally the infant sits with the parents while they communicate with each other. Each time the adult has to orient his/her body in the distance and closeness to the child that is specific for the situation. The infant is dependent on this parental frame, which guarantees its *participation* and abiding by its role in the play, so that it can keep its attention and is able to regulate its affects (F&C, p. 69).

As in any setting of communication such as this complex situation, miscoordinations occur too. The task of the triad principally consists of restoration of cooperation and (affect) attunement, so that it becomes possible to be together in a joyful way (F&C, p. 99). Without being interested in the participation of the others the organization and procedure of mutual play and regulation of affects do not succeed. The infant is an active partner in this, who tries to facilitate communication even between the three of them. Right from the beginning of the infant's life, successful cooperation of the parents with each other and with the infant is especially supportive of its development. For this to happen, it is relevant that the mother is interested in the involvement of the father, where she seems to have a "gate keeping" function. Her interest in the participation of the father depends on his sensitivity for the needs of the infant and her needs. Interestingly, the marital satisfaction of the fathers predicts the frequency of infants referencing to their fathers and the quantity and quality of his participation in parenting. The ability of the infant for the trilogue communication correlates to a high degree with this competence of the father. Males as husbands and fathers are more vulnerable to stress and conflict with their partners than are females as wives and mothers. (F&C, p. xxxix+175; Dornes 2006, p. 298+304). The stress sensitivity might be connected in some way to the differences in the oxytocin physiology of male and female (Uvnäs Moberg 2003, p. 5+176f.). It is: "interestingly enough, that coordination, whether of cells, effects, or individuals, is a marker for oxytocin" (ibid. p. 56).

As a consequence, missing participation of one (or more) partners of the triad may lead to disorganizing patterns of communication (and maybe attachment) and thus to severe disruption of the infant's self-development. (F&C, p. 50+76f.102; Klitzing 2002, p. 878). The growth, development and the future of infants are dependent on the cooperation of the parents. This

39

cooperation needs the participation of both parents as a couple with different mutual contributions due to different requirements interdependent of role differences and/or only for their special biological functions. For the development of the infant as well as the future of our society and higher order of intelligence, it is not the highly valued independence, competition and power that are beneficial but cooperation, touch, physical contact and love, which are often underestimated. (Cf. Uvnäs Moberg 2003, p. xi+177). Secure attachment grows with the sensitivity of the mother to comfort the baby and the sensitivity of the father in the play with the infant. The ability for triadic relations grows with triangulation of the parents in respectively cooperative family alliances (Dornes 2006, p. 318, tba.). Attachment and cooperative family alliances or collaboration now seem to be separate strands of development (E. Fivaz-Depeursinge, 2010, personal communication at the 12th world congress of the "World Association for Infant Mental Health [waimh] in Leipzig, Germany).

## 2.3. PHYSICAL HIERARCHY OF FAMILY COOPERATION AND THE GROUNDING CONCEPT

The evaluation of family cooperation research done with three and nine month olds as well as follow-ups of four-year-old children have been analyzed. The differing ability of parents to cooperate in so-called family alliances is already evident in the developmental stage of the basal or body core self (in two or three month old infants), and can be seen on four levels of physical interaction:

1.  Pelvis = *participation*: the *orientation of the lower body* to each other is foundational and crucial, whether all three partners in the relationship are included in the play (basic rootedness of social interactions).

2.  Torsos = organization: the relation of the upper body (shoulders) indicates, whether each partner is aware of his/her role (*turns to* the other in the appropriate distance).

3.  Gazes = focus of attention: the position of the head (direction of look) indicates whether all three partners are able to create a shared focus of attention.

4. Facial expression + voice = affective contact: expressive behavior indicates (analogous to dyadic play) whether each partner is able to initiate, develop and maintain affective contact and thereby emotional intimacy.

So in playing, the partners have to attune on differing physical levels. In doing so their lower body is placed in one spot and this position is kept as a rule. Their upper body is moved from time to time and has to be brought to the appropriate distance; head and look are newly oriented very often; facial expression, vocalization and other forms of expressive behavior change extremely quickly. Considered together, the four physical levels of interaction as hierarchical system form the triangular framing for play, affect attunement and development of the infant. Like in a developmental pyramid, the highest level of affective resonance is impossible without the previous levels of physical attunement: "The most encompassing and invariant components (the participation formations) exert a stronger influence on the least encompassing and most variant ones (the affective contact formations). We refer to the stronger forces as *contextual* and to the weaker forces as *implicative*" (F&C, p. 70). The *participation of the partners in the communication*, which is crucial in such a context, depends on the physical orientation of pelvis and legs for this to happen (the lower half of the body is connected with grounding). This basic framing of the play can be seen as a precondition for the later development of autonomy and grounding of the child. Thus the importance of the grounding concept is expanded by a developmental psychological perspective and dimension.

## 2.4. EFFECT OF DISRUPTIVE COOPERATION FOR CHILDHOOD DEVELOPMENT

The trilogue research has revealed two dysfunctional (*disordered and collusive*) frameworks of family alliances when parents have only low cooperative co-parenting and framing abilities for containment of interaction and play. So-called _disordered family alliances_ are characterized by a paradoxical relatedness (called *paradoxical triangulation*) with absurd corrections in the case of disruptions of attunement. Thus a participation of all three in the play is not possible, a collapse of co-operation is pre-programmed. The infant experiences *no participation* in shared interaction, but is helplessly exposed to the chaos of his parental environment. This means that already the *grounding*, the relation of the lower bodies with each other is disrupted. In that process the triadic abilities of the child are used and distorted in a paradoxical way (F&C, p. 102f.). Such chaotic relatedness with intrusion or withdrawal is also an indicator of the *disorganizing attachment style*. Disrupted family alliances may lead to the development of Borderline disorders. This would validate cooperation as an important independent category of intersubjectivity that follows its own separate strands of development. A recent investigation highlights the fact that, "individuals with BDP (borderline personality disorder) showed a profound incapacity to maintain cooperation, and were impaired in their ability to repair broken cooperation on the basis of a quantitative measure of coaxing" (King-Casas et al. 2008, cf. Schroeter 2009). How will these pieces of a puzzle fit together? Bioenergetic Analysis focusing on the physical dynamics and the cooperative strands of development might contribute to that puzzle (by focusing the cooperative or collaborative aspects in therapy).

In so-called *collusive family alliances* aggravating or evasive correction of miscoordination occurs caused by the parents. This leads to an affectively artificial context, which tries to maintain the appearance of cooperation (what later on might arise in alexithymia of adults). The (parentified) child from the beginning has the task to be the guardian of the unity of the parents as a couple. In order to prevent the disintegration of the connection of the triad, in these role-reversing families the child has to bring his own triangular capacities into service for triadic relatedness and affect regulation. The child has to provide for a frame for the conflicting and competing parental relations with a tremendous effort that is holding them together to pacify the parent's relationship. Receiving this framing from the parents would support the very important secure intergenerational boundaries with containment and holding for the baby. This form of cooperation is called *detouring triangulation* (F&C, p. 178f.). According to the insights resulting from the Lausanne-

Trilogue-Play the position of the upper body (torso) is connected with the organization or abidance by roles in relationships. In the course of the development of the infant's triangular capacities, the theme of exclusion from the parent's control field in its second year of life may be of special importance for these subgroups (Fivaz-Depeursinge et al. 2010, p. 137). If my considerations are conclusive, they might be helpful to explain the characteristics that can be observed in patients suffering from somatoform (and psychosomatic) disturbances: the therapist has to be especially careful to stick to his role, to his function as an empathic and supportive relational partner with clear boundaries, who provides for a frame. In this role he has to be authentic and to provide for information and knowledge (Morschitzky 2007).

## 2.5.    RELEVANCE OF RESEARCH

Research about the primary triangle is equally relevant for psychoanalysts as well as for body psychotherapists:
1.    Hierarchical physical foundations for patterns of communication are described in a differentiated way.
2.    Fonagy et. al. emphasize the significance of affect attunement and mentalization for the development of the self and its disturbances: "In this way in the core of their self structure (of the insecurely attached infant, author's note) the representation of the object becomes imprinted, not the one of the self" (Fonagy et al. 2004, p. 472). Their reflections may not take enough into consideration, that the core of the self-structure represents an embodiment of the relational experience from a time before the acquisition of symbolic representations (cf. Lichtenberg 1989, p. 87, Stern 2005, Sto., p. 86). Even Fonagy and his group seem to now take into consideration the importance of embodiment more (Fonagy&Target 2007). Schore (2005, p. 414) emphasizes more explicitly: "... the defensive response of the child to trauma, the regulatory strategy of this dissociation becomes imprinted in the implicit-procedural memory system of the right hemisphere." In considering the primary triad, the independent significance of the cooperative physical interaction becomes

an independent focus of attention in addition to the significance of affect attunement and attachment (F&C, p. 55f.). Both areas are of importance for the development of the infant and are following independent developmental lines (Downing 2007, p. 561).

3. Disruptions in the cooperation of the parents with each other and with the infant, already by the age of three months, verifiably lead to different relational patterns, so-called family alliances. The patterns (of disruption) of such family alliances are quite stable throughout the first year of life and lead to characteristic developmental disturbances, which are detectable in the infant in the fourth year of life.

4. For the development of the infant the interplay of "affective connection (affect attunement)" and "collaborative connection (or physical cooperation)" was shown by video microanalysis (F&C). The connective link between them seems to be represented by the physical hierarchy of the attunement processes. For a coherent self and adult functioning both strands of development have to cooperate in an integrated way.

5. Like attachment, the triangular or collaborative strand of development undergoes some changes in the growing up of the infant. The infant's triangular interactions precede rather than follow the advent of the oedipal complex. In the first year of its life the frustration of the infant in its triad dialogues is about a sense of *exclusion* from the parent's *attentional field*. The second year comes under the *exclusion* from the parent's *control field*, whereas from the third year on, it would concern the *exclusion* from the parent's *intimacy*. This points to the importance of the family alliance and of the infant's triangular capacity in determining the course of the child's sexual development (Fivaz-Depeursinge et al. 2010, p. 137).

## 2.6. PSYCHOTHERAPEUTIC SIGNIFICANCE OF RESULTS OF RESEARCH ABOUT FAMILY TRIADS

According to the considerations above, grounding understood in this developmental psychological psychosomatic sense means that the *par-*

*ticipation* of the partners in the interaction (also in the psychotherapeutic dyad) is necessary (what actually seems self-evident). This means specifically, that *physical* (hierarchically structured) *orientation can* be an important foundation for the *participation of the partners in mutual affect regulation.* The participation can be encouraged in the therapeutic work and by attentiveness to the perception of the lower half of the body. In this way Downing's (2007, p. 561) general description of the significance of the cooperation with the patient is substantiated. Patients with a coherent self and stable ego-functions have a sense of an inner security (or mental representation) of this participation, even independently of (implicit procedural) physical patterns of participation according to my experience. On the other hand, patients suffering from personality disorders with disturbances of self-representations, fragmentation or dissociation, depersonalization, derealization, and/or disturbances of body image for instance may be lacking those secure physical and psychological representations.

The following case example may demonstrate the applicability of these reflections:

CASE VIGNETTE 2: PHYSICAL PARTICIPATION AS FOUNDATION OF DEVELOPMENT AND HEALING

I am giving here an account of the still ongoing treatment of a patient with Borderline personality structure. She is 41 years of age, married for four years, and has an extramarital son of 19. After several interrupted attempts to begin her studies at university, she works as a physical-technical assistant.

*About her history*: She is the fourth of five children. Her mother has never overcome the death of a child that died shortly after birth and was born before the patient. The patient experiences her as if she would like to slip into her mother from behind like into overalls using a zipper, in order to be able to control her in this way. The father is a devout farmer. His motto: the human being is fundamentally evil and the devil has to be beaten out of him. As an infant the patient was often ill and suffered from behavioral disturbances and developmental retardation that led to many stays at a health resort.

For a long time the patient used the third person when she talked about herself. She felt easily drawn into public attention, exposed and shamed. With her conviction that everything about her was wrong, it was difficult for her to protect herself and she responded by freezing. She suffered from strong constrictions and pain on the right side of her body, especially in the area of the head and jaw, also from tinnitus, panic attacks and anhedonia. The sense of her right eye uncontrollably turning away by itself was particularly alarming for her. She complained about frequent cramps in her feet, while her extremities normally felt ice-cold. The father of her child had almost killed her during their separation. A girl friend who had been present during this situation had lost consciousness. The patient had survived the situation because of her dissociative processing capacities, in her words by "talking down" what had happened.

*All beginnings are difficult*: she had a hard time getting involved with therapy, with at first one or two, later on two or three weekly sessions. The curriculum vitae I had asked her for she wrote only a year later. Each communication meant stress and panic for her. Only after some progress in her therapy she was able to write to me about how much she hated her body and was ashamed of her-self and her body. Just talking about her body was like being physically touched. In the relationship with men, thoughts dominated which she called childlike and stubborn: "Who cares what he thinks, just let him hit me." Relational patterns like this occurred regularly in therapy, when she would hold her arm protectively over her head in panic. Then as a rule she had no memory of her written statements. "Intellectual knowledge" and "emotional experience" are dissociated.

Consequently she was extremely distrustful and at the same time expected that I simply sense her every inner stirring and know what she needs in each moment. She felt completely dependent on relational regulation by me without having any hope in participation. After some time she was able to illustrate her relational experience by means of a book and we found a comparison for her experience: "Like an Eskimo snow-child, that at the slightest inattention from my side will be left behind in the snowstorm and die miserably." When we had "survived" her feeling storms for a longer period of time, the need in her grew: "But first of all we have to make contact in the first place". After many attempts we ultimately found for that a frame that I had proposed: we sit facing each other at a distance, so that I am able to put my forefeet (without shoes) on her feet. We had also experimented with her feet on mine. Now she asks for this kind of contact at the beginning of each session. It has become informative for the whole process of therapy and establishes a physical relatedness, which according to her feeling does not come *too* close. Her participation in the relational dialogue is in this way is assured (as a rule). Even across difficult conflicts, she becomes rooted through her feet – as well in our relationship as on the ground. Abidance by the role, focus of attention and affective contact are still now and then disrupted depending on the intensity of tension – by turning away in the upper body, her look and closing of her eyes.

*Therapeutic dilemmas*: this kind of relational cooperation allowed us to keep the intensity of feeling again and again in a supportive middle realm. In strong tensions and when she was flooded by feelings the physical holding allowed her a piercing scream as a relieving expression. This was also for her a first tangible way to express protest and rage. She was thus less forced to dissociate or disrupt the connection, and to distort or turn away her upper body and the direction of her look less frequently. The setting and frame of the physical cooperation allowed also turning points or "now-moments" to arise. I mention here one of the most significant ones: during a bus ride three young women provoked a man with their giggling and screeching so much, that he "angrily had a go at them". In this moment the patient feared for her and their life. When I did not share her fear and indignation during her narration without reservations and asked questions, we happened to get into a similarly acute conflict. At the same time she abruptly discontinued our contact with the feet – for the first time –, placed her arms protectively over her neck like in a trance and physically contracted. This did awake me: I became aware of the fact, that I resembled the man on the bus (or was identified with him. Seen from a psychodynamic perspective she experienced me in the role of father or/and mother and was afraid of parental rage and attributions of guilt). But in contrast to her history we were able to re-establish our connection and cooperation. I asked her after a while, how she experienced the situation and myself. She had experienced me as angry and threatening, felt helplessly at my mercy and felt no more participation in the regulation of the relationship. After having told me about her experience it was vital for her, that I recognized *"my participation"* in what had happened – e.g. my angry feelings. In the following sessions she re-established contact with the feet. She referred to it as "melting in contact" (of the frozen snow-child with frozen icy feet).

After having worked through this episode she told me that she had perceived me for the first time as a person *separate* from herself with my own feelings and ambitions and told me that she was now increasingly frequently able to *remember*. She began to perceive her own angry affects in other relational constellations and then also toward the therapist – and she began to find words and meanings for her experience. Here is an example in her own words: "Where previously primarily was a war zone in absolute wasteland now sometimes a little house with a red roof, a little front garden with a little flower meadow happens to stand on/above ruins and bomb craters. It was hard work, to plough through the grey war zone. Very, very exhausting, because I fell into these bomb craters again and again. There were no living creatures at all, but just ice-cold wind and free expanse instead, no beginning and no end. There was *nothing* – no building material, no colors, no plants. However it went on, I do not know. Obviously I have decided to do something! …"

According to the research of F&C, parents allow the infant with their cooperative framing to participate in the formation of the relationship and to abide by its role. In similar ways the therapist can create a reliable frame of participation and role organization. In the case above, the contact with the feet helped to ensure the participation. Secure framing of participation allowed the patient also to accept, with the orientation of her upper body, implicitly the role organization and enabled her to engage in eye contact and affect attunement. In this way she was able to see (in a double sense) the propositions and efforts of the therapist as such and to remember (explicitly the relational experience). At the beginning of therapy she felt hardly involved, looked rarely at me, distorted her head and upper body and in this way was hardly able to create a common focus of attention. The relational context was then empty or dissociated and lacked any mutual regulation (Schore 2005, p. 454). Creation and maintenance of participation, role organization and focus of attention that by now are possible are an expression of a new experience of relationship and allows for affect attunement.

When interruptions of affect attunement occur by now cooperation is possible, so that relational continuity can be re-established. Conflictual situations between patient and therapist frequently are crucial in the course of therapy. An intersubjective perspective, that tries to understand relational events as co-created (Beebe & Lachmann 2004, Clauer 2007, Orange et al. 2001) enhances the ability to leave the circle of attributions and counter-attributions more easily, to ask the patient about her perspective and inquire into the own perspective of the therapist and/or share it in part if required. By that process of *"deconstruction of perspectives"*[5] of patient and therapist (Beucke 2008), both perspectives are valued and the therapist can recognize his involvement in the evolution of the situation (Clauer 2007). The patient than feels comprehended (understood) again and seen (mirrored) in her perspective. This invited her to *participate* – instead of making her feel powerless or helplessness with a lack of feeling of self-efficacy (agency), feelings that have been so familiar to her. Her statements indicate that she thus has had the chance to experience the therapist as a subject. Current therapeutic work with this patient more frequently takes place on an intersubjective level, and there are increasing moments of encounter from self to self.

From the above follows without constraint: that the experienced participation, the grounding of the patient in the therapeutic dialogue is the more relevant the more the patient appears to be suffering from personality disorders. Even attentiveness and case related formation of the setting of the therapy might be ways to facilitate or establish participation and cooperation.

## CASE VIGNETTE 3: DECONSTRUCTION ON THE LEVEL OF "MICRO PRACTICES"

A patient with depressive and dissociative symptoms had come for almost three years twice a week to therapy. In her youth she had been

---

5  A lovely prose description of the "perspectivity of consciousness" and deconstruction can be found in Ende (1960, p. 124f.) in the chapter on the "Scheinriese" (literally: a giant who only seems to be one), who shrinks to his normal size when approached.

abused by her father for years and had never had a sexual relationship with a man. After progress at the beginning, the therapy seemed to be stuck for almost one year in an impasse. The patient felt like she had hit a wall, previous progress seemed to be reverted, and she quickly gained weight again. Welcoming in the hallway of the office was accompanied every time by her strange giggle. Although we recognized the context of the hallway with the experience of abuse and in spite of thorough "verbal" exploration of her perceptions and fantasies, the giggling for her remained unclear and unchanged. Before one session it was particularly intense and we both seemed to be so irritated by it, that after a while I proposed to repeat the scene of salutation. We investigated it a couple of times – like in slow motion on a video. In doing so the patient finally sensed a defensive response during our handshake, as she felt pulled by me. Previously, neither of us had been aware of this slight pull. In the process she experienced the connection to her father, who had "drawn her in his cellar" and abused her. In contrast I experienced myself with a friendly inviting feeling towards her. After that she was able to show towards me a clear response of building borders with arms crossed and a clear "No, not (anymore) with me". In the times after that she experienced and repeated this again and again. Now she made developmental steps that reminded us of those of an adolescent girl. The giggling we understood now as an expression of her ambivalent feelings of "being drawn to" and she could then also show and experience a seductive quality. Now finally she also was able to work with "charge and contain" exercises (cf. Shapiro 2006). She gained a lot of profit from that regular work of changing her "flaccid" qualities both in the sessions and at home, which was not possible before the deconstruction process.

Our different experience of the situation of the salutation apparently had led to an unconscious impairment of collaboration and attunement. The exploration of the perspectives of patient and therapist, the "deconstruction" of the "how and where" of the bodily experience, and the exploration of the "physical micro-practices" facilitated a re-establishment and a new form of the (intersubjective) cooperation (Beucke 2008, Clauer 2009).

## PART 3: CLINICAL CONSEQUENCES

The body formations described in the frame of the family cooperation have systemic properties (cf. F&C, p. xl). They create (as for the infant) a foundation for the development of patients, without which the therapy primarily of patients suffering from personality disorders may be impeded. Even without clarity about these concepts and connections, most therapeutic modalities and therapists establish such a (hierarchically shaped) physical orientation with their patients. Psychoanalysis for example had to vary its standard procedure in the lying position without eye contact when working with patients suffering from personality disorders and in those cases works sitting position "face to face". This facilitates implicit unconscious affect attunement of the partners of the therapeutic relationship affected by facial expression, but also the possibility of the unconscious bodily attunement and orientation to each other. In psychoanalysis, however, in its classical form this is done without touch!

I tried here to illustrate that our therapeutic options and possibilities are expanded by knowing these physical organizing principles (according to mental organizing principles, Orange et al. 2001). I do regard the knowledge about the foundations of the processes of our physical attunement and the motivational interest of the infant into intersubjective collaboration as an expansion or differentiation of the motivational systems as described by Lichtenberg et al. (2000).

### 3.1. CONCLUSION

Therapeutic work on the subject of relational problems and conflicts (mainly with patients suffering from personality disorders) does certainly not only consist of the physical interactions described above. I would like to emphasize this explicitly. But the additional observation, consideration and use of the bioenergetic principles of the organization of bodily cooperation/collaboration and grounding can be helpful, both for beginnings of therapy, within the process and in difficult therapeutic situations. At the same time the deconstruction of the perspectives of patient and therapist can be helpful – not only on the level of thinking and affect attunement but also on the level of physical cooperation/micro-practices. In this way the participation of both of them in the interaction can be restored or ensured. Ultimately the main focus will be the interplay and integration of theses two levels of our experience of relation.

## REFERENCES

Ayres, A.J. (2002) Bausteine der kindlichen Entwicklung. Springer (4.Aufl., Berlin). Engl. Org. (1979): Sensory Integration and the child. Western Psychological Services.

Bauer, J. (2002): Das Gedächtnis des Körpers. Piper (München).

Beebe, B.; Lachmann, F. M. (2002): Infant Research and Adult Treatment: Co-Constructing Interactions. The Analytic Press (Hillsdale, NJ).

Belz-Knöferl, A.; Brown, M. (2006): Horizontales Grounding. In: Marlock, G.; Weiss, H. (Hg.): Handbuch der Körperpsychotherapie. Schattauer (Stuttgart) 699–708.

Beucke, H. (2008): Intersubjektivität. Die Dekonstruktion der Perspektiven von Patient und Therapeut. Forum Psychoanal 24, 3–15.

Bischoff, J. (2009): Schwarmforschung. Die Klugheit der Massen. Geo 07, 46–60.

Blakeslee, S., Blakeslee, M. (2007): The body has a mind of its own: how body maps in your brain help you do (almost) everything better. Random House (New York).

Buti-Zaccagnini, G. (2008): Affektive Beziehungen und Körperprozesse. In: Heinrich-Clauer, V. (Hg): Handbuch Bioenergetische Analyse. Psychosozial (Gießen) 151–160.

Clauer, J. (2003): Some Developmental Aspects of Body and Identity. Analytic-Imaginary Body Psychotherapy. Euro.J.Bioenerg.Anal. & Psychotherapy 1, 16–31.

Clauer, J. (2007): Embodied Comprehension: Treatment of Psychosomatic Disorders in Bioenergetic Analysis. Bioenergetic Analysis 17, 105–133. Dt.(2008): Verkörpertes (leiblich-seelisches) Begreifen: Die Behandlung psychosomatischer Erkrankungen in der Bioenergetischen Analyse. In: Heinrich-Clauer, V.(Hg): Handbuch Bioenergetische Analyse. Psychosozial (Gießen) 383–409.

Clauer, J. (2009): Zum Grounding-Konzept der Bioenergetischen Analyse. Neurobiologische und entwicklungspsychologische Grundlagen. Psychoanalyse & Körper 15/8. Jg., 79–102.

Clauer, J., Koemeda-Lutz, M. (2010, in Druck): Behandlung depressiver Erkrankungen in der Bioenergetischen Analyse. In: Röhricht, F. (Hg.): Störungsorientierte Körperpsychotherapie: Schulenspezifische Konzepte im Dialog. Psychosozial (Gießen).

Damasio, A. (2000): Ich fühle, also bin ich. List (München).

Dornes, M. (2006): Die Seele des Kindes: Entstehung und Entwicklung. Fischer (Frankfurt/M.).

Downing, G. (2007): Unbehagliche Anfänge: Wie man Psychotherapie mit schwierigen Patienten in Gang setzen kann. In: Geißler, P.; Heisterkamp,G. (Hg.): Psychoanalyse der Lebensbewegungen. Springer (Wien) 555–581.

Ehrensperger, T. P. (2006): Erdung in der therapeutischen Arbeit und im Alltag. In: Marlock, G., Weiss, H. (Hg.): Handbuch der Körperpsychotherapie. Schattauer (Stuttgart) 692–698.

Ende, M. (1960): Jim Knopf und Lukas der Lokomotivführer. Thienemann (Stuttgart).

Fivaz-Depeursinge, E.; Corboz-Warnery, A. (1999): The Primary Triangle. Basic Books (New York).

Fonagy, P.; György, G.; Elliot, L. J.; Target, M. (2004): Affektregulierung, Mentalisierung und die Entwicklung des Selbst. Klett-Cotta (Stuttgart).

Fonagy, P.; Target, M. (2007): The rooting of the mind in the body. J. Amer. Psychoanalytic Assoc. 55, 411–456.

Grafton, S. T. (2009): Embodied Cognition and the Simulation of Action to Understand Others. Ann. N. Y. Acad. Sci. 1156, 97–117.

Heinen, N.: Hirngespinste. Süddeutsche 116(2010), p. 24)

Heinrich, V. (1997): Körperliche Phänomene der Gegenübertragung – Therapeuten als Resonanzkörper: Welche Saiten geraten in Schwingung? (Intuitive Diagnostik). Forum Bioenergetic Analyse 1/97, 32–41. Engl. (1999): Physical Phenomena of Countertransference: Therapists as a Resonance Body. Bioenergetic Analysis 10(2), 19–31.

Heinrich, V. (2001): Übertragungs- und Gegenübertragungsbeziehung in der Körperpsychotherapie. Psychotherapy Forum 9, 62–70.

Heinrich-Clauer, V. (2008)(Hg.): Handbuch Bioenergetische Analyse. Psychosozial (Gießen).

Helfaer, P. M. (2007): Shame in the Light of Sex and Self-Respect. Bioenergetic Analysis 17, 57–79.

King-Casas, B.; Sharp, C.; Lomax-Bream, L.; Lohrenz, T.; Fonagy, P.; Montague, P. R. (2009): The Rupture and Repair of Cooperation in Borderline Personality Disorder. Science 321, 806–810.

Kushi, M. (1994); Do-In-Buch: Übungen zur körperlichen und geistigen Entwicklung. Mahajiva (Holthausen).

Lewis, R. (2008): Der Cephale Schock als Somatisches Verbindungsglied zur Persönlichkeit des Falschen Selbst. In: Heinrich-Clauer, V. (Hg.): Handbuch Bioenergetische Analyse. Psychosozial (Gießen). 113–128.

Lichtenberg, J. D. (1989): Modellszenen, Affekte und das Unbewußte. In: Kutter, P. (Hg.): Selbstpsychologie (2. Aufl.). Klett-Cotta (Stuttgart).

Lichtenberg, J. D.; Lachmann, F. M.; Fosshage, F. L. (2000): Das Selbst und die motivationalen Systeme. Brandes&Apsel (Frankfurt/M). Engl. (1992): Self and Motivational Systems. Toward a Theory of Psychoanalytic Technique. The Analytic Press (Hillsdale, NJ).

Lovejoy, O. (2009): Science

Lowen, A. (1978): Depression: Unsere Zeitkrankheit, Ursachen und Wege der Heilung. Kösel (München). Engl. (1972): Depression and the Body. Coward, McCann&Geoghegan (New York).

Lowen, A. (1983): Narcissism: Denial of the true Self. Macmillan (New York).

Lowen, A. (1986): A psychosomatic illness. Bioenergetic Analysis 2: 1–11.

Metzinger, T. (2005): Die Selbstmodell-Theorie der Subjektivität: Eine Kurzdarstellung in sechs Schritten. In: Herrmann, C.S.; Pauen, M.; Rieger, J.W.; Schicktanz, S. (Hg.): Bewusstsein: Philosophie, Neurowissenschaften, Ethik. UTB/Fink (München) 5–32.

Metzinger, T. (2009): The Ego Tunnel. The Science of the Mind and the Myth of the Self. Basic Books (New York).

Milch, W. (2001): Lehrbuch der Selbstpsychologie. Kohlhammer (Stuttgart).

Morschitzky, H. (2007): Somatoforme Störungen(2. Aufl.). Springer (Wien).

Oelmann, K. (1996): Grounding – Identitätsfindung als Bioenergetischer Analytiker. In: Ehrensperger T.P. (Hg.): Zwischen Himmel und Erde: Beiträge zum Grounding-Konzept. Basel (Schwabe) 129–142.

Orange, D.; Atwood, G.; Stolorow, R. (2001): Intersubjektivität in der Psychoanalyse: Kontextualismus in der psychoanalytischen Praxis. Brandes&Apsel (Frankfurt/M). Engl. (1997): Working Intersubjectively: Contextualism in Psychoanalytic Practice. The Analytic Press (Hillsdale,NJ).

Pechtl, W. (1980): Die Therapeutische Beziehung und die Funktion des Therapeuten in der Bioenergetischen Analyse. In: Petzold H. (Hg.): Die Rolle des Therapeuten und die therapeutische Beziehung. Junfermann (Paderborn) S. 189–210.

Reinert, T. (2007): Langzeitbehandlung bei Patienten mit Borderline-Störungen. In: Geißler, P., Heisterkamp,G. (Hg.): Psychoanalyse der Lebensbewegungen. Springer (Wien) S. 487–519.

Schore, A. (2002): Advances in Neuropsychoanalysis, Attachment Theory and Trauma Research: Implications for Self-Psychology. Psychoanalytic inquiry 22: 433–484.

Schroeter, V. (2009): Borderline Character Structure Revisited. Bioenergetic Analysis 19, p. 31–51.

Shapiro, B. (2006): Bioenergetic Boundary-Building. Bioenergetic Analysis 16, p. 155–178.

Steckel, H. (2006): Dynamisches Grounding – Containment und Selbstausdruck. Forum Bioenergetic Analyse 1/2006, S. 34–48.

Stern, D.N. (1985):

Stern, D.N. (2005): Der Gegenwartsmoment. Brandes&Apsel (Frankfurt/M). Engl. (2004): The Present Moment in Psychotherapy and Everyday Life. W.W. Norton (New York)

Storch, M.; Cantieni, B.; Hüther, G.; Tschacher, W. (2006): Embodiment: Die Wechselwirkung von Körper und Psyche verstehen und nutzen. Hans Huber (Bern).

Uvnäs Moberg, K. (2003): The Oxytocin Factor. Tapping the Hormone of Calm, Love and Healing. Da Capo Press (Cambridge, MA).

Winnicott, D.W. (1974): Reifungsprozesse und fördernde Umwelt. Fischer (Frankfurt/M). Engl. (1965): The Maturational Processes and the Facilitating Environment. The Hogarth Press (London).

## ABOUT THE AUTHOR

Dr. Jörg Clauer, born in Hamburg/Germany first became a biochemist and later a physician and medical doctor. He specialised in psychiatry, in psychosomatics and as a general practitioner. He started his psychotherapeutic education with Psychodrama, Bioenergetic Analysis (CBT) and with Body Enlightenment. Finally he became a Psychoanalyst and member of DPG and DGPT in Germany and IARPP as well. He has published articles on different subjects in a number of journals and books, for instance "Handbuch Bioenergetische Analyse" and is a member of the editorial stuff of the german journal "Forum der Bioenergetischen Analyse". For many years he was on the board of the Northern German Institute of Bioenergetic Analysis (NIBA) and was a founding member of the European Federation of Bioenergetic Analysis/Psychotherapy (EFBAP).

For many years he has been working in different psychosomatic clinics for indoor patients as co-Director. Since 1999 he has been working in a private psychotherapeutic practice, as a teacher and as a clinical supervisor for counsellors of couples and families.

He has a son and is living with his second wife, Dr. Vita Heinrich-Clauer in Osnabrück/North Germany.

Krahnstr. 17
49074 Osnabrück
Germany
+49 (0) 541-2023100
joerg.clauer@osnanet.de

# What Has Changed for Clients of the Bioenergetics Approach to Therapy in the Realm of Their Relationship with God?

*James L. Allard*

## Abstracts

### English

This article is an abridgement of a 112-page doctoral phenomenological research paper bearing the same title. The research was based on five case studies and answers the questions of whether and how Bioenergetics therapy influences one's relationship with God. Using John Conger's *Jung and Reich*, Jung's *Modern Man in Search of a Soul*, Alexander Lowen's *The Spirituality of the Body* and many other of their writings, it systematically compares the participants' testimonies to the literature concerning grounding, selfhood, relationship, love and faith. It also answers the question of who or what God is in parallel to what Jung, Reich and Lowen have written on the subject and explores the topic of the discovery of God through a connection with the body.

*Key Words:* love, trust, faith, God

## Was hat sich für KlientInnen, die mit bioenergetischer Analyse behandelt wurden, in ihrer Beziehung zu Gott verändert? (German)

Dieser Beitrag ist die Kurzfassung einer 112-seitigen Dissertation über ein phänomenologisch ausgerichtetes Forschungsprojekt mit demselben Titel. Die Untersuchung basiert auf fünf Fallstudien und beantwortet Fragen, ob und ggfs. wie Bioenergetische Therapie die persönliche Beziehung zu Gott beeinflusst. Unter Verwendung von John Congers *Jung and Reich*, Jungs *Modern Man in Search of a Soul*, Alexander Lowens *The Spirituality of the Body* und einer Reihe von anderen Schriften dieser Autoren vergleicht der Beitrag systematisch die Aussagen der StudienteilnehmerInnen mit der Literatur bezüglich Erdung, Selbstbewusstsein, Beziehungen, Liebe und Glaube. Er beantwortet auch die Frage, wer oder was Gott sei im Vergleich zu den schriftlichen Äußerungen von Jung, Reich und Lowen zu diesem Thema und untersucht die Frage, ob und wie Gott durch eine Verbindung zum Körper entdeckt werden kann.

*Schlüsselbegriffe:* Liebe, Vertrauen, Glaube, Gott

## Qu'est-ce qui a changé pour les clients de l'approche bioénergétique en thérapie dans le royaume de leur relation à Dieu (French)

Cet article est un résumé d'un article de Recherche phénoménologique doctoral de 112 pages portant le même titre. La recherche était basée sur l'étude de cinq cas et répond aux questions: si et comment la thérapie bioénergétique influence la relation de la personne à Dieu. En utilisant John Conger's *Jung and Reich*, Jung: *l'Homme Moderne à la Recherche de son Ame*, Alexander Lowen *la Spiritualité du Corps* et beaucoup d'autres de leurs écrits, il compare systématiquement les témoignages des participants à la littérature concernant l'enracinement, l'individualité, la relation, l'amour et la foi. Il répond aussi aux questions de qui ou quel Dieu est en parallèle à ce que Jung, Reich et Lowen ont écrit sur le sujet et explore le thème de la découverte de Dieu à travers une connexion avec le corps.

*Mots Cle:* Amour, Confiance, Foi, Dieu

## Qué ha cambiado para los clientes del Enfoque Bioenergético a la Terapia en la esfera de su Relación con Dios? (Spanish)

Este artículo es un resumen de una investigación fenomenológica de doctorado con el mismo título. La investigación se basó en el estudio de cinco casos y responde a las preguntas de si y cómo la terapia bioenergética influencia la relación de uno con Dios. Utilizando Jung and Reich, de John Conger, El hombre moderno en busca de su alma, de Jung, La espiritualidad del cuerpo, de Alexander Lowen y muchos otros de sus escritos, compara sistemáticamente los testimonios de los participantes con escritos referidos a los conceptos de enraizamiento, el sí mismo, la relación, el amor y la fe. Tambien da respuesta a la pregunta de quien o que Dios se corresponde con lo que Jung, Reich y Lowen han escrito sobre el tema y explora el tema del descubrimiento de Dios a través de la conexión con el cuerpo.

*Palabras Clave:* amor, confianza, fe, Dios

## Cosa è cambiato per i pazienti dell'approccio bioenergetico per quanto riguarda la loro relazione con Dio? (Italian)

Questo articolo è un'edizione ridotta di una tesi di dottorato basata su una ricerca con lo stesso titolo. La ricerca era basata su cinque casi e risponde alla domanda se e come la terapia bioenergetica influenzi la relazione con Dio. Utilizzando il libro di John Conger *Jung e Reich*, il libro di Jung *L'uomo moderno alla ricerca di Dio*, e *La Spiritualità e il corpo* di Lowen oltre a molti altri loro scritti, vengono sistematicamente comparate le testimonianze dei partecipanti con la letteratura sul *grounding*, il senso di Sé, la relazionalità, l'amore e la fede. Risponde anche alla domanda di chi o cosa sia Dio parallelamente a quanto hanno scritto Jung, Reich e Lowen sul tema, ed esplora l'argomento della scoperta di Dio attraverso la connessione con il corpo.

*Parole chiave:* amore, fiducia, fede, Dio

## O QUE MUDOU NOS CLIENTES DA ABORDAGEM TERAPÊUTICA BIOENERGÉTICA NA ESFERA DE SEU RELACIONAMENTO COM DEUS? (PORTOGUÊS)

Este artigo é um sumário de um documento de 112 páginas de pesquisa fenomenológica de doutorado com o mesmo título. A pesquisa foi baseada em cinco estudos de caso e responde às perguntas sobre se e como a terapia bioenergética influencia a relação com Deus.

Usando "Jung e Reich" de John Conger, "o Homem Moderno em busca de uma Alma" – de Jung, "A Espiritualidade do Corpo" de Alexander Lowen e muitos outros de seus escritos, ele compara sistematicamente os testemunhos dos participantes com a literatura sobre grounding, individualidade, relacionamento, amor e fé. Ele também responde a pergunta de quem ou qual Deus está em paralelo com o que Jung, Reich e Lowen escreveram sobre o tema e explora o tema da descoberta de Deus através de uma conexão com o corpo.

*Palavras chave:* amor, confiança, fé, Deus

## 1.0 INTRODUCTION

Given Lowen's (1990) thoughts on the subject of God, I wanted to explore what had changed for clients of Bioenergetics in the realm of their relationship with God. The project developed in the context of a doctoral program leading to a *Diplôme de 3ème cycle d'anthropologie spirituelle* at the *Université de Sherbrooke* in Sherbrooke, Québec, Canada. I noted statistics that confirmed an intuitive perception that religious practice had declined in my country over the course of 20 years whereas the use of alternative or complementary health care services including various forms of counselling therapies had increased. Were people looking for healing in their lives through a relationship with God via modalities other than organized religion? With Lowen's (1990) thoughts on the subject of God as background, this state of affairs moved me to want to explore further the subject of God in relation to Bioenergetics.

There was no particular hypothesis to prove, only a wish to explore and better understand the phenomenon called "God" (in our culture) in light of Bioenergetics theory and therapy. Hence, instead of the usual quantitative approach to research based on a hypothesis, I chose a particular type of qualitative research called the phenomenological approach. Out of my findings could result a hypothesis for further quantitative research but that would come later.

An ethics committee approved the research proposal in February 2008 and the data was collected in March and April 2008. The final report was submitted for evaluation and was accepted in December 2009. The complete text of the report covers 112 pages, including 54 pages of data, and can be found at the library of the university or can be found at either *Library and Archives Canada* in Ottawa or at the *Bibliothèque et Archives nationales du Québec* in Montréal under the title, "What Has Changed for Clients of the Bioenergetics Approach to Therapy in the Realm of Their Relationship With God?" and bearing ISBN 978-0-9866054-0-6.

## 1.1    The Theory

Reich (1973) postulates that man's distress might be attributed to his relationship to the cosmic energy that governs him. Conger (2005) points to Reich's idea that if the body were released from its armour, life would be immediately present and would be the answer to religious quest and hunger. Conger (2005) also states that Reich, the scientist and atheist throughout much of his life, discovered in the latter part of his life a spiritual orientation and experienced a direct intuitive apprehension of God, Life, Nature, Brahma, and Cosmic Orgone. To that effect Reich (1973) concludes that God exists as Reich becomes aware of the existence of an objective functional logic in the universe.

Jung (1933) states that a religious attitude is an element of psychic life whose importance cannot be overrated since many neuroses are caused by the fact that people blind themselves to their own religious promptings because of a passion for rational enlightenment. He notes that a truly religious person harbours a respect for the secret of human life and senses in everything the unseen presence of God. In his discussion about God, Jung (1973a) (Conger 2005) says though the God-image is a psychological fact, the psychologist cannot say anything about the metaphysical reality of God. Jung (1933) concludes that he cannot determine the nature of God and yet notes that while human beings resist learning that God is their father, successive generations who have understood what is meant by the fact that God is our father have arisen. Jung (1956) is of the opinion that psychic energy or libido creates the God-image by making use of the archetypal patterns contained in the collective unconscious. His conclusion is that the God-image is a real but subjective phenomenon. Jung (1973b) (Conger 2005) says that sexuality is of the greatest importance as the expression of the other face of God, the dark side of the God-image.

Jung (1933) recognizes the unity of body and spirit. Reich (1970) (Conger 2005) sees mind and body as functionally identical. Like Jung and in the wake of Reich, Lowen (1970) believes in the functional identity of mind and body. Jung (1933) acknowledges the modern tendency to view the psyche as primarily a product of the body but goes on to postulate that the psyche could instead arise from a spiritual principle which is as inaccessible to our understanding as matter. Jung (1933) equates the psyche with the soul, understood as the source of life and points to the fact that the word "soul" implies a moving or life force. Jung (1933) concludes, as does Lowen (1975; 1977), that breath and movement in a body are taken for life.

Lowen (1990) notes that human beings are viscerally connected to other living organisms and to Nature. Spirituality derives from that sense of connection to a force greater than ourselves. Lowen (1990) states that when a connection to the outer world is broken there is a parallel loss of connection with the bodily self as reflected in a loss of connection between the body segments, such loss of connection underlying both depression and the schizoid state. He points to when a conflict between a child and its parent becomes a power struggle, the loving connection between parent and child is broken resulting in a damaged spirituality for the child. He describes the mechanics of Nature for passing life from mother to child, refers to such mechanics as a loving connection, and views such as the initial model for connection in a person's life.

Lowen (1990) understands the process of making connections with the outside world as an energetic process and points to the feeling of being connected as absolutely vital to healthy life. He therefore understands energy as the basis for the body's spirituality. Consequently Bioenergetics is a form of treatment based on an understanding of the energetic processes in the body. Lowen (1990) notes the spirituality inherent in the body's urge to reach out. He defines spirit as a force that acts within us or through us, a force that has a mind of its own with an awareness that is deeper and broader than our consciousness, but also a force that is not recognized as the self. He notes that the spirit of a person is to be recognized in that person's unconscious and that such spirit is inherent in the living tissue of a person's body. For Lowen (1990) the spirit is like fire that transforms matter into energy, not the matter nor the energy but the process of transformation itself.

Lowen (1990) notes that a body's need for excitement gives rise to an impulse to reach out for contact with another body. But Lowen (1990) also speaks of a loss of connection, to God, life and Nature, through a drive for success to fulfill an underlying wish that was forfeited in the early relationship with parents, a wish to be loved. Lowen (1990) states that emotions are the direct expression of a person's spirit. But since emotions result from physical feeling in the body, feeling is the key to the spirituality of the body. Lowen (1990) sees in chronically tense muscles the body mechanics underlying the loss of feeling, and therefore underlying the loss of connection. He explains that the will underlying the drive for success separates the head from the body as it separates the individual from the community of fellow human beings or from identification with the universal. Lowen (1990) notes that the rigidity related to less feeling in a person's body parallels an increased brain activity to the point that the person derives a sense of self from the thought processes that are occurring instead of from feeling in the body. He describes control and faith as opposites.

Reminiscent of Jung's collective unconscious and of Reich's orgone energy, Lowen (1990) speaks of the pulsation at the core of one's being that unites one to the universe, of an animal soul in harmony with Nature. Lowen (1990) states that whatever means are used to establish a feeling connection to the infinite, it must involve the body if it is to be more than an idea in one's head. Says he, to become one with God, human beings must surrender their ego. Lowen sees in the heart, the organ that unites spirituality and sexuality. He notes how the heart, through the flow of blood, connects energetically the two ends of the body, the brain and the sexual or reproductive system, which represent the two opposing forces acting in the body, one that draws the organism upward and one that draws it downward. He introduces the idea of grounding as meaning the connection to reality, to one's body, to one's sexuality and to the people with whom one has relationships. Without grounding, a person's spirituality is a lifeless abstraction.

Lowen (1990) points to love, a deep heartfelt connection to another person or persons, to a different creature, to Nature or to God, as the essential nourishment to sustain the human spirit. Says he, love is a bodily feeling and faith a bodily attitude. An animal's faith is characterized by its unconscious acceptance that its world is right. Lowen (1990) points to faith as the state of being open and allowing the natural excitation to flow freely through one's body. Lowen (1990) recognizes a communion with God in the love felt in one's heart. He states that at the core of a body's operations lies the mystery of love. He points to the ability to feel a resonance between the pulse of the heart experienced in the feeling of love and the pulse of the universe as an indication that the heart is the temple where God resides in the human being.

Lowen (1990) states that the process of industrialization has gone so far as to undermine the faith of most people in the rightness of their world and in the existence of a beneficent force in the universe that would ensure their survival and well-being. He notes how in so many cases faith has turned a fatal prognosis into a seemingly miraculous cure and how such miracles are not due to mysterious forces from outside the body that can enter and cure illness. Says he, faith operates from within, though it may be evoked by an experience of love. Opening one's self to God's love has a very positive effect on the body through its exciting and expansive effect.

Lowen's (1990) description of human beings as connected to other living organisms and to Nature, as well as his description of Nature's mechanics for passing life from mother to child establish the grounds upon which the relationship essential for the attainment of selfhood needs to develop. A healthy relationship with mother brings about a healthy relationship with self, meaning self-awareness, self-expression and self-possession (Lowen 1985). In the counselling enterprise the relationship with a counsellor brings about a deepening of that relationship with self. Lowen's (1977) tools for a relationship with self are physical through body exercises but always in the context of a relationship with a counsellor. He recognizes a communion with God in the love felt in one's heart. Love is what is felt when life is passed on from mother to child. Faith is what develops through that love. A relationship with self therefore precedes a relationship with God and a relationship with self develops through a relationship with someone else.

## 2.0 METHODOLOGY

I interviewed five clients, their principal characteristic being that they had chosen to do therapy with this particular body-oriented approach. I chose them through the convenience of their availability for interviewing. All were female clients of the same female Certified Bioenergetic Therapist. To avoid influencing their answers, participants were told in broad terms that the gist of the research was to study their development in the realm of their relationship with God as a result of their investment of time and energy in therapy with Bioenergetics. I approached the question, **first of all,** by examining what had changed for these clients of the Bioenergetics approach to therapy in the realm of their relationship with self and, more specifically, in terms of self-awareness, self-expression and self-possession. **Secondly,** I examined what had changed for these clients in the realm of their relationship with others. **Finally,** I examined what had changed for these clients in the realm of their relationship with God. Regarding this latter aspect I introduced the subject by asking questions concerning love and faith in the lives of the persons interviewed while taking care not to define God in any particular way. I then asked these same persons to describe their relationship with God in a fashion that allowed them to define, in their words, their understanding of God.

**Participant 1** was a woman who would not be any more specific than to say that she was between 45 and 50 years of age. She had experienced approximately 160 sessions with Bioenergetics spread over four years. **Participant 2** was a 59 year-old woman who had experienced approximately 320 sessions with Bioenergetics spread over eight years. Prior to this, she had also experienced what she called "dream therapy" with another therapist for an undisclosed amount of time. **Participant 3** was a 64 year-old woman who had experienced over 245 sessions with Bioenergetics spread over nine years. She had originally begun therapy with a counsellor from an Employee Assistance Program who referred her to a female Bioenergetics therapist because she needed to feel "free to discuss more personal issues with a woman instead of with (a man)." She also had seen a psychiatrist because "doctors thought (she) should be on meds." The participant had also taken part in occasional workshops with two other female Bioenergetics therapists. **Participant 4** was a 46 year-old woman who had experienced approximately 90 sessions with Bioenergetics spread over three and one half years. Prior to Bioenergetics, she also "did talk therapy occasionally over the years." Finally, **Participant 5** was a 59 year-old woman who had experienced approximately 135 sessions with Bioenergetics spread over four and one half years.

Participants were solicited verbally for an audio recording of an interview. Their information was transcribed for the purpose of analysis. Questions were geared to the theoretical constructs of Lowen and can be found in section 2.1 of this article. The data was analysed based on Lowen's theoretical constructs occasionally augmented by constructs from Reich or Jung. The software Atlas.ti was used for the purposes of analysis.

## 2.1    INTERVIEW QUESTIONS

1.   If you refer to your original objective in therapy, what has changed in your life over the period that you have experienced therapy? Specifically:

a) What has changed in terms of awareness of your self?

b) What has changed in terms of whether you express your self or not?

c) What has changed in terms of how you express your self in the context of other people?

2. What has changed in your life over the period that you have experienced therapy in the realm of your relationship with others?

3. Over the period that you have experienced therapy, what has changed with regards to love in your life? Specifically:

a) What has changed with regards to feeling loved or cared for?

b) What has changed with regards to loving or caring for someone else?

4. Over the period that you have experienced therapy, what has changed with regards to trusting your own impulses?

5. What has changed in your life over the period that you have experienced therapy in the realm of your relationship with God? Specifically:

a) Describe your relationship with God before beginning therapy.

b) Describe your relationship with God currently.

c) Is there a particular event or happening in your therapy that stands out in the way that it influenced your relationship with God? Describe that event. What did you experience in that event that influenced your relationship with God?

## 3.0   THE RESULTS

The full report contains 54 pages of data, which, for the sake of brevity, cannot be reproduced in this article. The full data is available for public scrutiny by requesting the full report from the libraries mentioned in section 1.0.

The original study examined the aspects of grounding, selfhood, relationship with self and others, love, faith, and relationship with God for each of the five participants. In this article I describe only the essential elements of love, faith, and relationship with God, the latter aspect being developed as follows:

3.3  Who or What is God? Interpretation of the Data
3.4  Discover God through a Connection with the Body: Interpretation of the Data
3.5  Influence of an Event or Experience in Therapy on a Relationship with God
  A)  Summary of the Data
  B)  Interpretation of the Data
3.6  What Has Changed for Clients of the Bioenergetics Approach to Therapy in the Realm of Their Relationship with God: Summary of the Data (Only).

What follows is excerpted from the full report. Whenever quotes are used, the words contained within are taken directly from the participants.

## 3.1    LOVE: INTERPRETATION OF THE DATA

**Participant 1** felt loved by her animals before beginning therapy, an example of Lowen's (1990) idea that love can involve a connection to a different creature. **Participant 4** feels love as coming from "the Earth, (...) the Universe," an example of Lowen's (1990) idea of a connection to Nature, though the words used are different. **All participants** noted the love, care or support that they felt from their therapist or therapists. That love or care has allowed them to identify love from their families and others. Also, **all participants** have grown in their ability to love others. By mentioning their therapist and others as the source or the object of love, participants have confirmed Lowen's (1990) idea of love as a heartfelt connection to another person. Though there are still some areas of resistance, **Participants 1 through 4** have developed their ability to love themselves by accepting their emotions, illustrating Lowen's (1990) idea of a parallel between a connection to the outer world and a connection to the bodily self where the participants' connection to the outer world is seen in their relationship to their therapist. **Participant**

5 illustrates the same idea though less explicitly when she allows herself to receive love from her therapist, thus connecting to the outside world and simultaneously to herself.

**Participant 2's** childhood experience of having to "keep on working" because no one was going to support her, led her to become sick. This illustrates what Lowen (1990) meant when he spoke of a loss of connection, to God, life and Nature, through a drive for success to fulfill an underlying wish that was forfeited in the early relationship with parents, a wish to be loved. **Participant 4** illustrates Lowen's (1990) idea of a drive for success leading to the separation of the head from the body when she notes that she progressively came down into her body with Bioenergetics. I come to this conclusion by interpreting Participant 4's statements that she "worked out things on (her) own for a long time and relied on (herself) to figure things out," and that, for her, therapy was the opposite of "striving to be something or do something", as indications that she was driven to achieve success. Lowen's (1990) idea of the loss of connection resulting from a loss of feeling and in turn resulting in chronically tense muscles is the implicit conclusion that I derive from the fact that **all participants** experienced the body work of Bioenergetics exercises which are designed to reverse this process by releasing muscle tension and, concomitantly developing a connection to their therapist and to others.

## 3.2    FAITH (TRUST): INTERPRETATION OF THE DATA

Bioenergetics has enabled all participants to learn to trust their impulses, meaning that they have allowed the natural excitation of their body to flow freely in their body, which corresponds to Lowen's (1990) understanding of faith. In so doing, they have further developed their unconscious acceptance that their world is right, the characteristic that, according to Lowen (1990), defines an animal's faith. Lowen (1990) notes that faith operates from within and, indeed, by trusting their impulses participants have demonstrated that faith is a force that operates within the person.

**Participants 2 and 4** illustrate what Lowen (1990) means by the expression "faith (…) in the rightness of their world or in the existence of a beneficent force in the universe that would ensure their survival and well-being." Prior to therapy, Participant 2 feared "stopping doing," implying a lack of faith or trust in the World to take care of her and yet, with therapy, came "to trust that everything was OK." Participant 4 had "to let it all go and accept the fact that (she) may never come back," implying a trust or faith in such a beneficent force.

**Participant 4** illustrates Lowen's (1990) idea of a person deriving a sense of self from the thought processes that are occurring instead of from feeling in the body since throughout her life she tried to "figure things out analytically" whereas with Bioenergetics she tried to integrate "on a feeling level" what she knew intellectually. **Participant 5** illustrates Lowen's (1990) idea that control and faith are opposites when she "pays (…) more attention" to impulses that "don't sound that illogical but still (…) sound like a long shot" and appear "out of the blue" since control through logic is a product of the intellect.


### 3.3    WHO OR WHAT IS GOD? INTERPRETATION OF THE DATA

Although I did not ask a specific question concerning who or what God is, I found that participants implicitly addressed this topic as they answered other questions concerning their relationship with God. This section deals with the participants' current understanding of who or what God is, i.e. subsequent to therapy.

If at first sight **Participant 1** appears ambivalent in her understanding about who or what God is – is it spirit or is it what she sees in Nature that makes her feel good? – She tells of the therapeutic experience where she revealed the "monster" part of herself and as a result felt "at peace." She then says: "Maybe that was the day that I stopped hating God," and "Maybe God does love me even though I am a lesbian," and "Maybe He was really there for me." "God" is the word that she uses, as if, beyond the ambivalence of her intellectual understanding, she is trying to tell us that this was her experience of God.

**Participant 2** discovered that God communicates with her through her dreams. She has a sense that God is to be found inside rather than outside of herself, and in the people that she meets rather than "up there like a big judge." She uses words describing feeling to elaborate on her experience of God.

**Participant 3** left the confines of the definitions of God put forward by her denomination to find Him "outside the perimeters." She cannot define Him anymore but instead experiences Him "in the internal talking and the dialogue that (they) have together, and (in) the softening of His presence inside of (her), (meaning) that He accepts (her) in spite of the flaws that (her husband) and (her) kids and the Church and everyone believes that (she) has." She feels "there are moments (that) (...) He utterly delights in His creation of (her)." Finally, she notes how "amazing (it was) to know the sense of God's spirit" in a workshop where, according to the perimeter in which she was brought up, God would definitely not be present.

**Participant 4** intellectually defines God as "the energy or the essence of a person" but then she recognizes God in "the expression of" "loving someone else" "despite (...) the more unattractive parts of being human." She adds that "God fits in with love and compassion and how (she) feels towards other people," insinuating a lived experience. She further and more strongly implies a lived experience when she says: "As I accept myself more wholly, I'm able to accept the other person more wholly." Like for the other participants, I find Participant 4's best definition of whom or what God is when I pay attention to her lived experience.

**Participant 5** has "no idea (of) whom or what God is" but feeling more connected to her physical reality "feels compatible with whatever God is." She recognizes God as an energy that she feels as vibration in her body. She recognizes God through "a physical experience of (...) creatively intelligent power," a "felt phenomenon, (...) not just (...) an idea." Her experience of God is as if "everything (she) has known in (her) head becomes real in (her) body" such that her body feels something that is "not separate anymore" from her thought. Of an experience where she felt an "incredible kindness" in her therapist's eyes she says that such "had to do with a relationship with God in the same sense of immanence."

Each participant speaks of the presence of God in an experience of love, confirming Lowen's (1990) idea that a communion with God is to be seen in the love felt in one's heart. **Participant 1** felt "at peace" and says: "Maybe God does love me"; **Participant 2** speaks of her experience of God as a "caring" presence in her life; **Participant 3** speaks of feeling accepted by God and of God delighting in her; **Participant 4** says: "God fits in with love and compassion and how I feel towards other people"; **Participant 5** notes the "incredible kindness" that she felt in her therapist's eyes and how such "had to do with a relationship with God in the same sense of immanence."

Also, Lowen's (1990) idea that to become one with God, human beings must surrender their ego, is reflected in the participants' experience with Bioenergetics whose stated purpose (Lowen 1971, 1970) is to soften the chronic tension in the musculature, i. e. to surrender the ego, in order to honour the pleasure principle of the id. Participants surrendered their ego and, as noted previously, felt the presence of God.

Finally, Lowen (1990) speaks of spirit as a force that acts within us or through us, a force that has a mind of its own with an awareness that is deeper and broader than our consciousness. On the other hand, Beauregard and O'Leary (2007) describe the effects on the brain of a mystical condition in which the subjects said, "they felt the presence of God, his unconditional and infinite love, and plenitude and peace." Though the authors add that the subjects, "also felt a surrendering to God," they clarify that their findings do not prove nor disprove that mystics contact a power outside of themselves. Despite this clarification, they nevertheless conclude: "The data are consistent with an experience in which the experiencers contact a spiritual reality outside of their own minds." As noted earlier, each participant speaks of the presence of God in an experience of love. Given that Beauregard and O'Leary's (2007) research results are "consistent with an experience in which the experiencers contact a spiritual reality outside of their own minds," I conclude, using Lowen's (1990) definition, that it is plausible to think of God, "as a force that acts within us or through us, a force that has a mind of its own with an awareness that is deeper and broader than our consciousness" but different from ourselves. Such a statement is as much as can be said in answering the question of who or what God is, and is consistent with Jung's (1973a) (Conger, 2005) view that though the God-image is a psychological fact, the psychologist cannot say anything about the metaphysical reality of God.

## 3.4 Discover God through a Connection with the Body: Interpretation of the Data

**Participant 1** sees in Nature, "Spirit's way or (…) God's way of showing (her) more love." She sees it in rainbows; she speaks of hawks and eagles as her "spiritual guides"; "there to help (her)". She watches them "flying around," "filling (her) up with (…) freedom". She feels "amazed" when watching a chickadee at a bird feeder feeding himself. She finds it "mind boggling" to see "a blue jay (…) out in the middle of a snow storm in a tree in the middle of" a large city. If she sees these things now, Participant 1 did not see them before Bioenergetics therapy. She relates to God through the different actions that feel like love or feel like beauty in the World. To reconcile herself with the ugliness that she sometimes sees in the World, she "stops thinking godlike and (instead) thinks just what (she's) receiving from the earth is spirit."

**Participant 2** senses that "God's in here (as she points to herself) rather than out there" and "feels like God is (…) all around (her) in the people (she) meets rather than God's up there like a big judge." She understands her dreams as her "own customized scriptures" implying a communication from God from within, and she brings her dreams to Bioenergetics because, "the dreams are from (her) body anyways," meaning that a connection with God happens through the body. She "needed the Bioenergetics to really become comfortable in (her) own skin that (…) (she) was fine with God and God was fine with (her)," again pointing to a connection with God through feeling in the body. It makes sense to her that Jesus would heal someone's blindness, whether on the Sabbath or otherwise, meaning that she relates to God through what feels right in her body, for example, the healing of someone's blindness. And it does not make sense to her that God would tell Abraham to kill his only son on an altar, again meaning that she relates to God through what feels right in her body.

**Participant 3** is "very conscious of flickering moments" when she "knows of (God's) presence inside of (herself)," as she feels "great joy and peace." Noting some remaining resistance to accepting that God loves her, she nevertheless points to the effect of the physical exercises of Bioenergetics in that they "have softened (her) into a place of acceptance," meaning that the softening in her body is bringing her closer to God. Noting her initial dread of the mattress as a Bioenergetics instrument of exercise, she now "doesn't mind being on the mattress and doing the exercises that (she) needs to do for whatever aspect (she) is in on that day." Of this fact she says that God is "opening up another area in (her) life (that she) hasn't ever explored," meaning that she is relating to God by exploring "whatever aspect (for which she) is in on that day" through the physical exercises on the mattress. Prior to therapy, for Participant 3, "sexuality would have been a bad thing because it got you in trouble." Through the Bioenergetics exercises, she learned to allow her sexual feelings to rise and, as a consequence, recognizes that her relationship with God has changed thus, again, indicating a relationship with God through a connection with the body.

"Therapy has brought (**Participant 4**) back to (her) body" where she realises that she is "part of the One (…) Universal Energy, One Consciousness, whatever." It has also brought her the realisation that she can "access God more through (her) feelings or (…) (her) body." Bioenergetics exercises helped her "work through (her) anxiety physically, on a body level" and, in turn, find the "calm or peace" that she was seeking and find God through feeling "more secure in the world." Further illustrating how she discovered God through a connection with her body, Participant 4 tells of reading a book concerning "the wisdom of the Earth," which, in turn, motivated her "to focus more on just being grounded in the world." And, since she felt "so much comfort and peace being around trees in (…) the forest, (…) (she) just started being more aware of those things and less being rattled in (her) head." Finally, Participant 4 finds God when she "quiets (herself) and just looks really, really deep inside."

With Bioenergetics therapy, **Participant 5** has "moved closer to being able to integrate a sort of concept or idea of God with (…) a sort of living experience or even (with) physical feelings that (she) identifies as God," though she is not there yet. She recognizes God as an energy that she feels as vibration in her body. Of her experience of God, she says it is "like everything (she) has known in (her) head becomes real in (her) body." Her body feels something that is "not separate anymore" from her thought, in fact her body experience "affirms" what she has thought.

Participant 5 feels "more alive, (…) more in (her) body, (…) more on this Earth, (…) more aware physically of weight, of tension, of resistance, of connection, (and of) things like that (…) that (previously) weren't (…) part of (her) relationship with God."

All participants attest that they find God through a body experience, the result of working with Bioenergetics, which, since they find God through the life that they feel as a result of releasing the armour, illustrates Reich's idea that if the body were released from its armour, life would immediately be present and would be the answer to religious quest. They also illustrate Lowen's (1990) idea that whatever means are used to establish a feeling connection to the infinite, it must involve the body. **Participant 1** relates to God through the different actions that feel like love or feel like beauty in the World, implying that she has softened her armour and is thus able to feel. **Participant 2** discovers God in her dreams, which "are from her body anyways," and discovers God inside of herself and others. She relates to God through what feels right in her body. **Participant 3** recognizes God's "presence inside of (herself)" when she feels "great joy and peace." She discovers God through the Bioenergetics exercises that allow her to open up "another area in (her) life (that she) hasn't ever explored" before. Bioenergetics exercises helped **Participant 4** "work through (her) anxiety physically, on a body level" and, in turn, find the "calm or peace" that she was seeking and find God through feeling "more secure in the world." **Participant 5** recognizes God as an energy that she feels as vibration in her body. She is "more aware physically of weight, of tension, of resistance, of connection, (and of) things like that (…) that (previously) weren't part of (her) relationship with God."

## 3.5    INFLUENCE OF AN EVENT OR EXPERIENCE IN THERAPY ON A RELATIONSHIP WITH GOD

### A) SUMMARY OF THE DATA

The therapeutic event or experience that most influenced **Participant 1** in her relationship with God took place when she "just looked at (her therapist) and (…) (speaking of a hidden part of herself) said: 'It's time for you to meet this monster.' At that moment she accepted the "monster" part of herself, felt "at peace," and "stopped hating God." **Participant 2** points to the fact of integrating a sense of acceptance of herself from feeling accepted by her therapists as the most important factor that influenced her relationship with God. She specifically notes that her Bioenergetics therapist accompanied her to her preliminary Court hearing where she opposed a speeding ticket that she had received. To her, it was as if her mother had accompanied her. She felt secure. As her perception of the judge changed so did her perception of God. For **Participant 3** it was more of an experience than a single happening in therapy that influenced her most in her relationship with God. She credits the acceptance that she felt from her therapists. She also notes that with the Bioenergetics exercises she learned to allow her sexual feelings to rise. "(She) could honour that part of (her) being as something that was good and right and holy, not as something dirty, unclean, and (that) should (be done) (…) as quickly as possible and got over with." She points to her attendance at a workshop offered in a Catholic spirituality centre where, contrary to her expectation, she felt "amazed" by the care she sensed from others towards her. The single most significant experience that influenced **Participant 4** in her relationship with God is the grounding that "brought (her) (…) back to (her) body." It was during the first six months of her therapy, when she explored her anxiety and thus allowed herself to feel even "more anxious," that grounding had the most impact. She was further motivated "to focus more on just being grounded in the world" upon reading a book concerning "the wisdom of the Earth." The event in therapy that most influenced **Participant 5** in her relationship with God took place when, as her therapist asked her to look into her eyes, she suddenly thought, "my mother never looked at me like that." She felt in her therapist's eyes an "incredible kindness, (…) and a patience, and a willingness to be silent." She also notes as another factor that influenced her in her relationship with God, the reassuring "guidance" that she felt from her therapist when she, for the first time, felt the vibration in the back of her legs.

## B) INTERPRETATION OF THE DATA

The theme of acceptance underlies the event or experience that, in all five participants, most influenced the relationship with God. **Partici-**

pant 1 accepted the "monster" part of herself thus allowing herself to stop hating God, the backdrop being the acceptance that she felt from her therapist. **Participant 2** felt accepted by her therapists, which, in turn, helped her face a judge and change her perception about that judge, thus allowing her to change her perception of God. **Participant 3** felt accepted by her therapists and more specifically, in regards to her sexual feelings. She also felt cared for in a workshop where she did not expect such a thing to happen. **Participant 4** singles out the grounding that "brought (her) (...) back to (her) body" i.e. allowed her to accept herself, again the backdrop being the acceptance that she felt from her therapist who introduced her to grounding. **Participant 5** felt in her therapist's eyes the kindness, and patience that meant she was accepted.

## 3.6 WHAT HAS CHANGED FOR CLIENTS OF THE BIOENERGETICS APPROACH TO THERAPY IN THE REALM OF THEIR RELATIONSHIP WITH GOD: SUMMARY OF THE DATA

**Participant 1's** relationship with God prior to therapy was influenced by her "understanding that (...) (she) was a sinner and (...) would go to hell" because of her lesbian lifestyle and that "there was no turning back." As a result of Bioenergetics therapy she relates to God through the different actions that feel like love or feel like beauty in the World. In particular, she sees in Nature "Spirit's way or (...) God's way of showing (her) more love." She "sees love and spirit in a bird flying or when there's an ice storm and (one) is standing beside a tree that's making creaky noises". She sees "spirit moving in rainbows". She watches hawks and eagles "flying around" and that "fills (her) up with (...) freedom". She feels "amazed" when watching a chickadee at a bird feeder feeding himself. She speaks of birds, especially hawks, as her "guides" since she sees "a lot of red-tailed hawks." With therapy, and particularly after a specific cathartic event, Participant 1 concluded that "something's definitely watching over (...) (her)." She has "stopped worrying that everything (she) thought and did was a sin."

**Participant 2's** childhood experience was of a "very punitive" father such that God was seen as "something out there (...) who is going to be more punitive than loving." She compares her childhood experience of God to a Courtroom judge who could send her to jail. As a child, "God would seem to be unpredictable" to her. Her experience of God subsequent to therapy is of a "softer, (...) gentler, more feminine (...), caring, less remote (...), closer, warmer (...), less distant and less (...) unpredictable" presence in her life. Contrary to her upbringing in a "fundamentalist family (where) there were big things (they) weren't allowed to do (on) Sunday," Participant 2 demonstrates her current freedom when she reacts with, "Well, so what!" to an Old Testament rule that one was not to heal someone on the Sabbath. In one particular biblical story concerning Abraham being told to offer his son on an altar, she does not feel threatened anymore by something she does not understand. Subsequent to therapy Participant 2's experience of God is that God is to be found inside of herself rather than outside of herself, "wanting to punish (her)."

She feels accepted by God, and she recognizes God's action in her life and her occasional blindness to it.

For **Participant 3**, in the past God was "a God of harshness and rules that were to be kept." If Participant 3 "could fix a picture of Him before," now she cannot define Him anymore. "He no longer has perimeters in (her) world." To know God Participant 3 now has "to go outside the perimeters." In particular, prior to therapy, God's perimeter was such that He "was outside of sexuality" meaning that her experience of sexuality was filled with "guilt (...) (and to be) within the perimeters (...) of marriage." However, through the Bioenergetics exercises she "became aware of (her) sexuality, (and aware) that (she) was a sexual being," and sexuality became "a guilt free pleasure." Prior to therapy, though God was "supposed to be" in her, Participant 3 kept Him "at arms' length" but as she experienced therapy, especially Bioenergetics, she concluded that God is "not so far away as he used to be." In her words: "I know He is within me." Participant 3 has also "come into the place where (she) believes God actually does love (her) as an individual." Finally, as a result of therapy, Participant 3 "can be honest before (God)." If she is "thinking something that in (her) world would be bad or not something (she) should be thinking about," she can now say, "God, this is really how I'm feeling about this."

Subsequent to therapy **Participant 4** recognizes a different relationship with God from the fact that "the relationship with (herself) (...) has changed." She further recognizes a different relationship with God in the fact that she is able to be more compassionate towards others but says that is even more so the case as she develops a greater compassion for herself. She always believed "there was something else" but, prior to therapy, that "something else" came through "the traditional 'God in the sky' type thing (...) and Adam and Eve and all that kind of stuff." On the other hand, therapy has brought her the realisation that she can "access God more through (her) feelings or (...) (her) body." Rather than through "thinking about God," she now finds God when she "quiets (herself) and just looks really, really deep inside." The Bioenergetics exercises brought her back to her body and helped her find the "calm or peace" that she was seeking, and thus find God through feeling "more secure in the world."

**Participant 5's** relationship with God prior to Bioenergetics therapy was a "thoughtful, verbal (...) relationship of prayer, of talking, of asking, of thanking." It was "all head things, (...) not physically experiencing in (a) visceral way." Now she feels "more alive, (...) more in (her) body, (...) more on this Earth, (...) more aware physically of weight, of tension, of resistance, of connection, (and of) things like that (...) that (previously) weren't (...) part of (her) relationship with God." She notes a major shift in the way that she recognizes God. "It's not that (her) idea about God has shifted, (...) it's just now it has more integrity." Her feeling and her idea about God are now "simultaneous." With therapy she has "discovered (...) God (...) in a kind of (...) reality that wasn't there before," a reality that she "can viscerally experience." She has "moved closer to being able to integrate a sort of concept or idea of God with (...) a sort of living experience or even (with) physical feelings that (she) identifies as God," though she is not there yet.

## 4.0 DISCUSSION

Nowhere is the word "God" defined in this research. This was a conscious choice, allowing instead a common cultural background to implicitly define the word without words, and thus appealing to each participant's internal definition of the word. Cultural backgrounds of participants could obviously have been explored and thus the results of those findings could have been further correlated to the results of the study. Instead the assumption was that participants' cultural backgrounds were similar and, though religious instruction may have varied, were largely influenced by a prevalent Judaeo-Christian culture. Bioenergetics was born from and developed in a Judaeo-Christian culture. Lowen was Jewish. An extension of this study could therefore involve interviewing participants and therapists who come from non-Judaeo-Christian cultures.

All participants were women and all participants worked with the same female Bioenergetics therapist. Research with an equal number of male clients could therefore be considered in order to compare the results by gender. Research with a male Bioenergetics therapist could also be considered to ascertain if the gender of the therapist is a contributing factor in the results. The situation could also be made more complex by considering male clients with a female Bioenergetics therapist and female clients with a male Bioenergetics therapist. The results obtained from clients of one Bioenergetics therapist could also be compared to the results obtained from clients of another Bioenergetics therapist, in the hopes of ascertaining if individual therapists have an impact on the results.

Although Bioenergetics subscribes to no particular religious denomination and proposes no particular religious view other than what is exposed in this document concerning its understanding of God, another consideration would be the religious background of the Bioenergetics therapist. Does the religious background of the therapist enter the therapeutic relationship, if not consciously, at least subconsciously? And then, does the religious background of the participants affect the therapeutic relationship? In this research neither the religious background of the Bioenergetics therapist nor the religious background of the participants were explored except incidentally. Also, the Bioenergetics therapist whose clients I interviewed clearly stated that she in no way ever attempted to influence her clients' religious beliefs.

This research set out to elucidate the participants' experience of God or not, based on Lowen's understanding of God, and subsequent to experiencing Bioenergetics therapy. It was exploratory research, qualitative in nature, and for that reason was accomplished with a phenomenological approach. Besides contributing data for the understanding of the phenomenon referred to as "God" in our culture, my hope is to, through this article, stimulate discussion and/or further research. As for me, I am satisfied with the definition of God that I arrived at in section 3.3, which is based on Lowen's (1990) definition of spirit, Beauregard and O'Leary's (2007) research results and the data collected from the five participants in this study. It is possible to create hypotheses concerning the subject of God with variables that we can control (for example, gender of clients and therapists; or religious backgrounds of clients and therapists; or cultural backgrounds of clients and therapists etc.) and therefore to produce quantifiable data. However my understanding of Lowen's (1990) idea about God is that God is defined by an experience, not by a yardstick. I prefer therefore to invest my energy at understanding the phenomenon of "God" through the phenomenological approach, a particular type of qualitative research, rather than the quantitative approach to research. Two questions remain for further exploration. Is the phenomenon of "God" simply one to be noted or are there ways that this phenomenon can be helpful to the therapeutic process? And, are there approaches other than the accepted physical approaches of Bioenergetics that we can use to tap in to the phenomenon of "God" in order to help the therapeutic process?

This study has demonstrated that the five participants interviewed found God through a body experience, the result of working with Bioenergetics. Though this study applies to Bioenergetics, the immediate implications of its findings concerning the way to find God are for pastors in their ministry and theologians in their discourse about God rather than for therapists. Statistics demonstrate a decrease in religious practice and an increase in the use of alternative health care services. The questions that instead concern therapists and particularly Bioenergetics therapists revolve around whether and how we can further help the therapeutic process by referring to God.

My purpose as a researcher was not to prove nor disprove the existence of God but rather to document the phenomenon of "God" as experienced or not by clients of Bioenergetics.

## References

BEAUREGARD, M., & O'LEARY, D., (2007): The Spiritual Brain. HarperOne. New York.
CONGER, J., (2005): Jung and Reich. North Atlantic Books. Berkeley.
JUNG, C., (1973a): "Letter to Pastor Ernst Jahn, September 7, 1935" in C.G. Jung Letters. Translated by R.F.C. Hull.

Edited by Gerhard Adler and Aniela Jaffé. Bollingen Series XCV, vol. 1 (1906–1950). Princeton University Press. Princeton.

JUNG, C., (1973b): Memories, Dreams, Reflections, Revised edition. Translated by Richard and Clara Winston. Edited by Aniela Jaffé. Pantheon. New York.

JUNG, C., (1933): Modern Man in Search of a Soul. Translated by W.S. Dell and Cary F. Baynes. Harvest. New York.

JUNG, C., (1956): Symbols of Transformation: An Analysis of the Prelude to a Case of Schizophrenia, 2 edition. Translated by R.F.C. Hull. Bollingen Series XX, vol. 5. Princeton University Press. Princeton.

LOWEN, A., (1975): Bioenergetics. Penguin Books. London. LOWEN, A., (1971): The Language of the Body. Collier Books. New York. LOWEN, A., (1985): Narcissism: Denial of the True Self. Collier Books. New York. LOWEN, A., (1970): Pleasure. Penguin. New York. LOWEN, A., (1990): The Spirituality of the Body. MacMillan. New York.

LOWEN, A., (1977): The Way to Vibrant Health. Harper & Row Publishers. New York.

REICH, W., (1973): Cosmic Superimposition. Translated by Mary Boyd Higgins and Therese Pol. Farrar, Strauss & Giroux. New York.

REICH, W., (1970): The Function of the Orgasm. Translated by Theodore P. Wolfe. Meridian. New York.

## ABOUT THE AUTHOR

James Allard is a *Canadian Certified Counsellor* and a *Registered Counselling Therapist* practising in Nova Scotia. He completed two undergraduate degrees at the Université de Sherbrooke, in *Science* (1975) and in *Theology* (1983). He graduated with a *Master of Education (Counselling)* (1995) degree from Acadia University. He recently graduated from the Université de Sherbrooke's doctoral program in *Spiritual Anthropology* (2009). He is a *Certified Bioenergetic Therapist* (2004).

James L. Allard M.Ed., D.A.S. (3ème cycle), CBT
6025 Binney Street
Halifax, Nova Scotia B3H 2C2
Canada
(902) 425-1690
james.allard@usherbrooke.ca
www.bodymindtherapy.ca

# Broken and Veiled in Shame

## Revealed by the Body's Implicit Light[1]

*Robert Lewis*

## Abstracts

### English

This paper was a keynote presentation at the 2009 IIBA Conference on the Poetry of the Body in Buzios Brazil. It is proposed that we bioenergetic therapists are artisans whose craft is both an art form and a clinical science. In support of this thesis, the following questions are explored:

Is it possible to both celebrate the poetry and ineffable mystery of our work, and yet to remain true to and to honor our Reichian and Lowenian roots?

Can we be grounded in the mystery of life, without slipping into the "mystification" against which Reich warned us?

Has the 'grace of self' that we seek to 'unveil', actually evolved from the core pulsation which our founders strove to liberate from our character armor?

*Key Words:* mystery, broken, genital embrace, pulsation

---

1 This paper is taken from a keynote presentation at the IIBA conference, whose theme was, *Unveiling the Poetry of the Body*, and held in Buzios, Brazil, 2009.

## Fragmentiert und verhüllt durch Scham – entschleiert durch das implizite Licht des Körpers (German)

Dieser Beitrag ist die überarbeitete Version eines Hauptvortrags anlässlich der IIBA-Konferenz 2009 mit dem Leitthema "Poesie des Körpers" in Buzios, Brasilien. Es wird vorgeschlagen, Bioenergetische AnalytikerInnen als Handwerker zu betrachten, deren Handwerk sowohl eine Kunstform als auch eine klinische Wissenschaft darstellt. Zur Untermauerung dieser These werden folgende Fragen untersucht:

Ist es möglich, die Poesie und das unbeschreibliche Mysterium unserer Arbeit zu feiern und dabei gleichzeitig unseren Reichianischen und Lowenianischen Wurzeln treu zu bleiben und diese in Ehren zu halten?

Können wir im Mysterium des Lebens geerdet sein, ohne in "Mystifikationen" zu verfallen, vor denen uns Reich gewarnt hat?

Hat sich die "Anmut des Selbst", die wir zu entschleiern versuchen, tatsächlich aus den pulsierenden Bewegungen unseres inneren Kerns heraus entwickelt, die unsere Gründerväter vom Charakterpanzer zu befreien suchten?

*Schlüsselbegriffe:* Mysterium, fragmentiert, genitale Umarmung, Pulsation

## Casse et cache dans la honte. Revelee par la lumiere implicite du corps (French)

Cet article a été la conférence d'introduction du congrès 2009 de l'IIBA sur la Poésie du Corps à Buzios, Brésil. Il est proposé que, nous thérapeutes bioénergéticiens soyons des artisans dont le métier est une forme d'art (et) en même temps qu'une science clinique. A l'appui de cette thèse, les questions suivantes sont explorées:

Est il possible de célébrer à la fois la poésie et le mystère ineffable de notre travail et, en même temps, rester fidèle et honorer nos racines Reichiennes et Loweniennes?

Pouvons nous être enracinés dans le mystère de la vie sans "glisser" dans la "mystification" contre laquelle Reich nous a prévenu?

"La grâce du self" que nous cherchons à «dévoiler», s'est-elle développée à partir de la pulsation du centre que nos fondateurs ont tenté de libérer de notre armure caractérielle?

*Mots Cles:* Mystère, dévoiler, grâce, bioénergétiques, étreinte génitale, vague, pulsation, cassé

### Roto y velade en la verguenza. Revelado por la luz implícita del cuerpo (Spanish)

Este artículo se basa en la ponencia presentada en el Congreso del IIBA del 2009, La Poesía del Cuerpo, en Buzios, Brasil. En ella desarrollo la propuesta de que los analistas bioenergéticos somos artesanos cuya habilidad es a la vez una forma de arte y una ciencia clínica. Para apoyar esta tesis, se exploran las siguientes preguntas:

Es posible celebrar a la vez la poesía y el misterio inefable de nuestro trabajo y a la vez mantener y honrar nuestras raíces Reichianas y Lowenianas?

Podemos estar enraizados en el misterio de la vida, sin deslizarnos hacia la "mistificación" contra la cual Reich nos advirtió?

"La gracia del self que buscamos" "desvelar" ha evolucionado desde la pulsación nuclear que nuestros fundadores lucharon por liberar de nuestra armadura de carácter?

*Palabras Clave:* Misterio, roto, abrazo genital, pulsación

### Spezzato e nascosto dalla vergogna. Rivelato dalla implicita luce del corpo (Italian)

Questo articolo riprende la relazione presentata al Congresso dell'Iiba del 2009 a Buzios in Brasile. Vi si propone che noi analisti bioenergetici siamo artigiani la cui opera è sia una forma di arte che una scienza clinica. A sostegno di questa tesi, sono esplorate le seguenti questioni:

È possibile celebrare la poesia e l'ineffabile mistero del nostro lavoro, restare nel vero e onorare le nostre radici loweniane e reichiane? Possiamo essere radicati nel mistero della vita, senza scivolare nella "mistificazione" contro cui Reich ci messo in guardia? La "grazia del Sé" che cerchiamo di "svelare", in realtà si sviluppa dalla pulsazione del core che i nostri fondatori hanno lottato perché fosse liberata dall'armatura caratteriale?

*Parole chiave:* Mistero, spezzato, rapporto sessuale, pulsazione

### Derrotado e escondido de vergonha. Revelado pela luz implícita do corpo (Portuguese)

Este artigo foi uma apresentação na abertura da Conferência de 2009 do IIBA – Poesia do Corpo – Buzios, Brasil. Propõe-se que nós terapeutas bioenergéticos sejamos artesãos cujo ofício é uma forma de arte e uma ciência clínica. Em apoio a esta tese, as seguintes questões são abordadas:

Será possível que celebremos a poesia e o mistério inefável de nosso trabalho, e ao mesmo tempo ainda permaneçamos fiéis à honra e às nossas raízes Reichiana e Loweniana?

Podemos ser fundamentados no mistério da vida, sem resvalar para a "mistificação" contra a qual Reich nos preveniu?

Será que a "graça do self" que procuramos revelar, realmente evolui a partir da pulsação vinda do núcleo, aquela que nossos fundadores se dedicaram a liberar das armaduras de nosso caráter?

*Palavras chave:* Mistério, derrotado, enlace genital, pulsação

### The Real Work

It may be that when we no longer know what to do
we have come to our real work,
and that when we no longer know which way to go

we have come to our real journey.
The mind that is not baffled is not employed.

The impeded stream is the one that sings.

*Wendell Berry*


## INTRODUCTION

Our conference theme is quite wonderful. It was obviously chosen by
the Brazilian alchemists on the scientific committee. Like a great poem,
it delivers a deep truth in a deceptively simple way. It sings of the art
form that is therapy. It tells us that we therapists are artisan/artists. That
is, we are skilled craftsmen and women. Different in some ways from
the artist who creates his work of art, we learn to tune to the tone and
rhythm and pain and gesture of the body's poetry, and in so doing, our
patients' inner spirit is slowly revealed- unveiled to us. The other side
of this, however, is that what is unveiled/created in our therapy sessions
is actually co-created: it is deeply interactive and can be described as
two limbic systems in dialogue. The grace of self has a lot to do with
who is doing the unveiling. As the poet Yeats put it, "O body swayed
to music, O brightening glance, How can we know the dancer from the
dance?" (p. 217)
    So we are artisans whose craft is both an art form and a clinical science.
Is it possible to both celebrate the poetry and ineffable mystery of our
work, and yet to remain true to and honor our Reichian and Lowenian
roots? Can we be grounded in the mystery of life, without slipping into
the "mystification" against which Reich warned us? Has the 'grace of
self', which we seek to 'unveil', actually evolved from the core pulsation
which our founders strove to liberate from our character armor?
    Body in Poetry: with these three words the Scientific Committee,
perhaps with the help of the alchemically gifted god Hermes/Mercury,
have challenged an older scientific/medical left brain view. From this
mainstream perspective, the body is a complex piece of machinery that
has no relation to poetry. With these four words, I believe they both

honor our Reichian and Lowenian roots and incorporate recent research in neuroscience on the right brain that supports the current evolution of our bioenergetic craft. The "poetry of the body" is a poetically rendered metaphor/simile that crosses a boundary and invites us to make hidden connections.

But let us reflect further on the theme of our conference. Why, you may ask, is "the poetry of the body" such a powerful title? Suppose we were to change just one word and the title became "the prose of the body". Not good, you say, because, as we all know, as prose spells things out, it often becomes matter-of-fact. Indeed in English, the word prosaic means not fanciful or imaginative, not challenging and lacking in excitement. So let me return us to poetry of the body and grace of self and share with you what I really love about our theme. You see, I am happiest when the truth can barely be glimpsed in the twilight. Too much illumination kills the magic and mystery. When it comes to our theme, I believe I am not alone, because I am suggesting that poetry, grace of self and a living body are all finally ineffable – that is, they are beyond our grasp. Both grace and poetry, for instance, have so many varying definitions because they are probably indefinable. Kenneth Koch, a poet himself, puts it well:

> "Poetry is often regarded as a mystery, and in some respects it is one. No one is quite sure where poetry comes from, no one is quite sure exactly what it is, and no one knows, really, how anyone is able to write it."

Simply said, you can listen to the wind or to someone's soulful cry, but you cannot grasp, or fully comprehend them.

## FINDING LIGHT HERE IN THE DARKNESS

But I can almost hear you asking – how did Bob start with the lovely conference theme and arrive at a keynote topic of "broken and veiled in shame?" I have four answers. First, the mythological explanation: my muse and my chosen god, is Hermes/Mercury – god of contradictions and paradox. He is, in truth, actually my co-therapist. Thus, any talk inspired by Hermes could only be about the alchemy of graceful shame and shameful grace.

A second more profane reason is that I am a recovering wounded healer speaking to an audience of mostly recovering healers. Therefore the limbic and autonomic nervous systems of most of us in the room today do **not** tell a story of a self unveiled in grace. Hopefully we are more gracious today than we were when we emerged from our families of origin. But how many of us, like the Wizard of Oz, are still ashamed to be seen behind our professional personas for the people we really are in our private lives? I, for one, often catch myself trying too hard to be of value to my patients. I assume that at such times I am not feeling very valuable, certainly not gracious, as the human being that I am. Those of us who find this wounded healer talk discouraging, may be comforted by the message of Akiro Kurosawa in his film Rashomon. He tells us that we are not alone:

> "Human beings are unable to be honest with themselves about themselves. They cannot talk about themselves without embellishing. This script (Rashomon) portrays such human beings – the kind who cannot survive without lies to make them feel they are better people than they really are" (p. 183).

A third and related reason is that with such beautiful words as poetry and grace, it is easy enough to forget that the poetic form which best describes the embodied pain and loss of many of our patients is the elegy … in this case, the mournful lament for their own loss of life.

When I wrote this speech, the fourth reason that came to me was that I had just finished reading Paulo Coelho's, The Alchemist. I am not sure that I understand the connection. I believe that it was Coelho's telling us that:

"There is only one thing that makes a dream impossible to achieve: the fear of failure" (p. 141). So, on the way to success and grace, it is good to remember our failures. Coelho is certainly candid about the core shame and inadequacy that has been part of his inspiration. I hope he would agree that we are saved from hubris – excessive pride in our work as artisans, when we remember the many we have not helped as much as we and they had hoped, and when we remember that the best work we have done occurred when we surrendered to the wisdom in our (broken) hearts.

But let us get down to work and try to define the indefinable. What is grace, for instance? Here is a very short story about grace and a quality of mercy:

A mother sent her young daughter, aged 6 or 7, to her father's study one morning to deliver an important message. Shortly thereafter the daughter came back and said, "I'm sorry mother, the angel won't let me go in." Whereupon, the mother sent the daughter back a second time, with the same result. At this point the mother became quite annoyed at her young girl's imaginative excess, so she marched the message over to the father herself. Upon entering, she found the father dead in his study (Kalshed 1996, p. 41 – see Edinger 1986).

This story of the little girl and the angel brings home to me that when we are broken by life's traumas, this happens partly because some wisdom in us mercifully breaks up our cohesive wholeness so that the flame within us does not go out – so that our indomitable spirit can live on. Like the little girl in the story, we are born with a grace of self, and it scatters our spirit to the wind and armors our body until – by the awful grace of God – some day in the future – our life becomes safe enough to live the poetry of our body. So I am finding a wisdom and dignity in our brokenness along side of the shame.

Two of the many definitions of grace that I found are (1) a generosity of spirit and (2) mercy or clemency. I am quite certain that it is our generosity of spirit or graciousness as human beings, which enables us to witness the unveiling of grace of self in our patients. But first let me call on Shakespeare to help us illuminate grace. I myself felt a quality of mercy in the grace that delivered the angel to the little girl in the story I just read to you. Shakespeare (in Portia's soliloquy in the Merchant of Venice) tells us that:

> The quality of mercy is not strained
> It droppeth as the gentle rain from heaven
> Upon the place beneath. It is twice blest:
> It blesseth him that gives and him that takes
> (p. 111, lines 180–184)

Thus, in this way mercy is akin to the seemingly effortless beauty of movement, proportion and behavior which conveys grace and which we call gracious. And whether we ourselves experience or we witness a moment of unveiling, when body and spirit become one, we are indeed, as Shakespeare tells us "twice blest."

So bioenergetics has always been about the grace and poetry of our animal selves. Being grounded in one's sexuality and surrendering to the mystery of life, actually go hand in hand. It is not given to us to know exactly how the little girl found her angel. When it is given to us to witness such stories of survival, it is because something in our patient senses that we are a fellow human being who is safe enough and they then grace us by dropping the veil a bit.

We see, then, that bioenergetic artisans do not unveil people. The present participle "unveiling" in the conference title makes clear the obvious fact that we are never a finished product that can be fully understood as long as we are alive and as I put it some years ago ... as long as there is spirit to our bodies and body to our spirits. We remember that grace is something freely given, but like the mysterious essence of a poem or a human being, though it may be unveiled for a moment and received by us, we cannot grasp it too strongly, we cannot know it too fully. Most of us delighted, for instance, as children in the game of hiding and being found. Our patients still want us to find them. But when they have been broken and shamed, we must indeed be both wise and gracious to know how to visit them in the inner place where their core grace is shadowed by torment and isolation.

But why has it taken all these years and the Brazilian culture (forgive me for reducing this vast and vital country to one culture) to declare the body in poetry? I believe this has to do with the powerful personalities of Wilhelm Reich and Alexander Lowen. Both men were at their best when illuminating what had been in the shadows. But poetry and grace, as I have said, do not lend themselves to full illumination. Thus, I believe that in deference to the certitude of our founders, we have shied away from the ineffable.

Al set an example for all of us in how he both remained deeply true to his Reichian roots and yet did not canonize/mummify Reich's teachings. Rather, he infused them with his own creative inspiration. Now, with his passing, we can, as a living body of artisans, honor Al best by reaching for a bioenergetic institute that moves from and is inspired both by what Al inherited from Reich, what he added to the bioenergetic work in progress and what we each in turn bring to it.

In spite of our differences, what I do hope we all share and what Scott Baum described as foundational in his recent inaugural presidential message (IIBA Spring 2008 newsletter) to us, is a commitment to keeping our patients' (and our own) somatopsychic unity or lack of it, at the heart of our clinical encounters. This was Reich's enduring gift to us: the functional identity of a person's character and his bodily attitude. It will not go out of style.

But there is a sober reality facing us. It is possible, but not likely, that someone will emerge from among us post-Lowenian bioenergeticists who will be able to lead us with the force of certainty about his or her truth that emanated from Reich and Lowen. I doubt that anyone will ever match Al's passion for and genius at knowing a person in and from the pulse of their body. In fact, it was part of the genius of both men that they saw the life of the body with such a powerful and explicit light.

It will therefore be interesting to see what kind of therapeutic outcomes and unforeseen partnerships may arise as our patients sense that, even though we do the best we can to read in their psyche-soma the person that they are, we cannot see into their deepest recesses with the same conviction in the clarity of our vision that Reich and Lowen had. Sensing that we need help to unveil the mystery that they are, our patients may have to engage with us in a slow, implicit, mutual process of discovery.

Having said this, let me contradict myself at once, and urge you to read the chapter by Reich called the "genital embrace" (Reich, 1976) in his book "the Murder of Christ". I will quote a few lines which reveal a poetic nature that is not often seen in the rest of Reich's voluminous writings. He tells of the delight in the growing surrender to and discovery of embodied intimacy:

> "It takes many months, sometimes years, to learn to know your love partner in the body. The finding of the body of the beloved one itself is gratification of the first order ... this search itself and the mutual wordless

finding one's way into the beloved's sensations and truly cosmic quivering, is pure delight, clean like water in a mountain brook ... The growing itself, the constant experience of a new step, the discovery of a new kind of look, the revelation of another feature in the partner's make-up, no matter whether pleasant or unpleasant, in itself is great delight" (pp. 37–38).

So, after all, there is poetry in our Reichian roots and there is even the mystery of why Reich was unable to reveal more of the poetry that was in his heart. But let me unveil some of my **own** issues with poetry. I like to play with words, and I like to play with the obscure and complex in people. But I am no good at poetry. I am thinking of two poems that I have read numerous times and that are somehow too much for me. They are probably similar in this way to patients to whom I was not much help because I could not bear the pain and poetry in their hearts. The first poem is by John Milton, "On His Blindness". I present the first two lines of his sonnet:

> "When I consider how my light is spent,
> Ere half my days, in this dark world and wide ... "
> (p. 84)

The fact that this man lives in darkness and that I cannot fully grasp his words, brings his blindness too close to me. It is true that some of his references require knowledge of the Scriptures and his personal history to be explicitly understood. But my discomfort, as I have said, is with how Milton's rhythm and meter and words implicitly pull me too close to darkness. I was trained as a physician to tolerate the awful physical afflictions of life, but I am still afraid of the dark. And I was more or less also trained as a psychiatrist and bioenergetic therapist to be able to tolerate the awful emotional, spiritual and mental afflictions of life, but I am still afraid of the dark.

So when the embodied poems in my patients are too dark for me, I sometimes flee into my left brain and insist on a bright, explicit light. But as we know, grace comes unbidden. So as I, still baffled but hopeful, once more submit myself to the last few lines of Milton's sonnet, they bring me light. He says:

*God doth not need*
*Either man's work or his own gifts: who best bear*
*His mild yoke, they serve him best ...*
*They also serve who only stand and wait.*
(p. 84)

Milton was a deeply religious man who feared that his blindness would
prevent him from adequately serving his God. Like many wounded
healers, I struggle with a kind of religious zeal to adequately serve my
patients and thereby feel less damaged, more whole. So, in the famous
last line of his sonnet, we learn again from Milton what we learn from
each patient – that we are somehow most healing when we embrace our
blindness and our brokenness.

The second poem is "The Little Black Boy" by William Blake. I will
read a few stanzas. The black boy's mother is speaking to him:

*And we are put on earth a little space,*
*That we may learn to bear the beams of love;*
*And these black bodies and this sunburnt face*
*Are but a cloud and like a shady grove.*

*For when our souls have learned the heat to bear,*
*The cloud will vanish, we shall hear His voice,*
*Saying, 'Come out from the grove, my love and care,*
*And round my golden tent like lambs rejoice.'*
(p. 9)

The poem continues, but if I allow myself to feel the two stanzas I
have just read to you, the ecstatic love is too heart breaking. So to
approach and really step into the sacred grove with our patients –
to the anguished places where there may still be some hope – how
do we do it? Personally, in some ways I find it easier to share my
failure and brokenness, than to reveal my power, my Trickster, my
magic, poetry and grace. As I already said, my inner Hermes has
been a friend for years. At first I just asked him to hide my shame by
seeing to it that people did not laugh **at** me but rather **with** me. But
over the years he has been doing some kind of alchemy that allows

my laughter to come from closer to my heart while still protecting my dignity.

Let me tell you a little story about how the alchemist does his quiet work with me and with my patient Paul. Paul, a very sad lonely patient of mine in his early forties, was lamenting with self-loathing that, in the past fifteen years, not only had he never had sex other than with a prostitute, but that he had **never** had whatever it took to suggest a sexual liaison to any woman. For some minutes as we sat quietly, I felt something like pity for Paul i. e., "wow, what an awful problem **he** has". His story was well beyond any conscious sense I had of my own masculine self. But over some minutes our two limbic systems had a silent talk, and my more shameful story came to light. I remembered how paralyzed with fear I had been as an adolescent – too frightened to kiss my first girlfriend – terrified of the rejection of my heartfelt erotic impulse which was the painful poetry that had been engrained in my young body. I remember then feeling much closer to Paul – as to a wounded brother. But I was far too ashamed to tell him about my painful recollection. I have no videos of that session, now some dozen years ago, but I doubt that a video would have fully captured the change in the implicit dance, in the poetry of our bodies, which occurred between Paul and myself. In English, we say, "don't just stand there, do something!" In our case, we did not even have to get out of our chairs.

But I know there was a lot of movement going on inside of me, and there is an immense amount of clinical research suggesting that our breathing, our matching of bodily attitude, our mutual gaze pattern and the music beneath our silences all reflect our shared vulnerable space in those silent moments. This was early in Paul's therapy and he might have been burdened by explicit knowledge of my sad story – he might have needed to hold on to some illusions about me in order to feed his hope. Here is where we healers need to be truly gracious: to sense how much our patient needs to know about the all too human soul to whom they have entrusted their healing. Thank God, as with our children, our patients sense, often in spite of our efforts, much more about who we really are than we realize.

## CORRESPONDENCES

There are many ways in which, when we are wise, we approach our patients the way we approach a poem. Modern neuroscience increasingly validates our bioenergetic view of the human organism. It calls our attention to the limitations of explicit symbolic language in conveying the essence, the heart and soul of a person. Often, out of awareness, our body sends implicit messages. Sometimes, they lead to instant insights, at other times we are only able to see their shape and hear their sound slowly as they emerge from the inchoate shadows. A gentle pulsation becomes a poignant gesture. A whispered breath becomes a heartfelt murmur. As our 'grace of self' is thus 'unveiled', our respiratory wave – little by little – embraces our head, our heart, our pelvis and the earth. So we are never that far from the hidden grace of self as it resonates in our inner pulsation. We sense its presence as our micro-tremors become spontaneous gestures. We try to sense what body tissues, organs, flows and blocks produce what movements and sounds from the different selves within us.

The tone and shape and flow of the body's shame, betrayal, the heart's forgiveness, it's spastic pain, its sweet erotic pulsation … these are the metre, paradox, metaphor and quatrain of the body's poetry.

In both the body and poetry there is a complex, intuitive dance between form and content that can be glimpsed for moments, but never be fully seen in the light of day. The body tells a story – by how it moves and breathes and how it is still. It embodies the story of what it has lived. If we are to approach our patients' bodies as the poems that they are, then we will begin by accepting that, like the body of any deep poem, they tell a story that is much more than we can ever fully know. How could it be otherwise, since, as we wounded healers know, our patients have come to us to help them with a pain that has been more than they could bear.

Those of us who have been artisans of this healing craft for some years know that we have done very well for our patients if we have been able to help them face and tolerate some good measure of the trauma that broke their wholeness. If this happens, it happens slowly. Like the poem that we read again and again, discovering together what pieces of the embodied poem, of our selves in pieces, that we can be with.

So the story with its terrible pain and shame has been more or less frozen in our character armor. Wilhelm Reich taught us that. Some of us may be able to see quite a bit of the story in our patient's body, but the patient will feel no more of it than what he can tolerate of the pain and shame that broke him in the first place. Much of the story, the poem, remains in the shadows, the unconscious, the implicit. The muted breathing, tight musculature, misaligned body segments – in themselves tormenting – also mercifully destroy meaning. The lights go out on the unthinkable loss of our selves.

## CLINICAL VIGNETTES

### FIRST VIGNETTE

Quite a few years ago, as I watched Al Lowen doing a demonstration session, he put his hand over the left chest of the patient and commented that one could make pretty direct contact with the patient's heart – I found the comment both obvious and startlingly powerful. As you know, that was often a signature quality of Al's comments.

Recently, after a break of several years, I was once again working with my now 50 year old patient, Paul, whose earlier session I just shared with you. As we worked, my hands found their way over his left chest. This had happened every now and then, and my patient always found some kind of deep comfort from it. A few months prior, it had in fact triggered a deep, sweet experience of melting into a state of loving feeling that was both new to Paul and very moving to me. This time, however, when I touched him, it led to him feeling a barrier covering his heart and he said angrily, "I am not going to cooperate – won't give you what you want. I'll do it when I'm ready" … This was followed by, "but I do feel the value of what you are doing – don't give up on me – I don't want to be left alone". After some moments, he said, "you must be a valuable human being … I've always thought of you more as an excellent therapist". I said, "perhaps you are also a valuable human being". After a silence, he said, "Doing this kind of work must be quite moving for you". I said,

"Yes, it is". Paul later said that the word that came closest to capturing this moment was: "humanity". But words do not quite capture this man's soul coming to the surface of his being and enveloping us in its poetry. Al Lowen, via bioenergetic analysis gave me (us) this and similar kinds of clinical 'now moments' in which we are privileged to directly touch the living body such that we unveil the grace of self.

## Listening to the Silence

THE POETRY OF THE BODY EXTENDS TO ITS MUSIC AND DANCE – we surrender to the story that is told by its gesture – the question it raises with the slightest quiver of an eyebrow – we are **informed by the many sounds that can be found in its many silences.** If we are patient and attentive to the void, to the body's darkness, it lights our way – shows (unveils to) us meanings that illuminate even as they remain obscure, The improbable becomes familiar. The light suffuses and water and oil become one.

## Second Vignette

When I hear my patient's voice as partially blocked/strangled and I sense that she is on the threshold of coming into the room with a more vulnerable, spontaneous sound, I sometimes massage the front of her throat – often at the thyro-hyoid membrane (a fibrous, membranous sheet filling the gap between the hyoid bone and the thyroid cartilage). I usually do this with a sense that I am going in to find or perhaps inviting out a traumatically fractured part of my patient's self. I tend to assume that I will be able to tolerate this part of them that is strangled within and thus help them to unveil some grace of self. But I often get ahead of myself and the poetry of my patient's body surprises me.

For instance, the cry of my patient, Anna, is strangled. Wendell Berry tells us that, "the impeded stream is the one that sings." Wendell is wise, but silence, like darkness, is strong poetry: neither of them tell you exactly which way to go and what to do. If I really listen to Anna with my whole body, I can feel something beckon. I can feel the sound that I cannot quite hear. When she falls silent, I am afraid to fall with her … there is no familiar form to hold onto … afraid to fall too far into the right brain. When I hear her broken, cracked voice that does not yield to a deeper sobbing, I feel an ache in my heart and grow frustrated. Why can't this woman trust that I can tolerate and will not recoil from her broken heart? Then she falls silent … in the sudden quiet … can I trust my senses? Did I hear some tone rising up from her heart? This partial deafness, this lack of clarity, pulls me once more too close to Milton's dark world. I am not sure, for instance, if Anna meets my gaze, what shades of feeling (emotion) might be dancing across my face in response to her silent song (music). What if her impeded stream of life sings not only of a broken heart, but of an ecstatic love that long ago her father could not bear and she now needs me to receive. Has my own broken heart healed enough so that I can bear her loving me now … so that I can bear the heat and beams of love that made William Blake's poem too ecstatic for me. If not, then Anna and I may both be blessed that her angel is silently, graciously holding both her heartbreak and her ecstatic love until we both can better bear them.

## THIRD VIGNETTE

I will close with the last of three clinical vignettes to illustrate the body's implicit light creating a space in which shame and grace wash over and into each other. On the surface, the stories seem quite different. I first worked with Sam at a Bioenergetic Conference about 5 years ago in a "demonstration session". I "knew" almost nothing of his story. As I stood face to face with this powerfully built man and we exchanged a few words, I sensed a dark, ominous presence. This was not the first time I remember wondering how I had gotten myself into a situation where I was likely to fail and make a fool of myself. I would say that the crucial feature of my intervention was that in spite of feeling quite small, something told me that it was alright to step closer and make physical contact with this threatening, but tormented man. What happened then and in two subsequent sessions recently is too complicated to do justice to here, but I want to quote some of Sam's own words to give you a sense of the poetry in body that happened:

First, some context: Sam had been an ordained priest. His family came from Lebanon. The words "guilt and shame" seem inadequate to describe the profound sense of unredeemable black damnation that was his torment. His call to the priesthood was in part a failed attempt to find that redemption via rising above his body and its sexuality. Sam explains:

> "As we worked and you encountered me – I was holding onto your right elbow, and you my left forearm – I had an impulse to grab you around your chest. As I grabbed you, you grabbed me in the same manner. My sense afterwards was that I could have crushed you in a bear hug and thrown you across the room. But with you matching me, I felt held by a loving human embrace and I was able to drop and surrender to a deep sobbing grief, and then rise up into a mutual joy with you at what we had accomplished."

I did not make a conscious decision to touch Sam because he felt untouchable i.e., hopelessly damned due to his darkly evil body and sexuality. Rather, our limbic systems silently cast a suffusing light on each other – and I was told (by my intuition) what to do. Poetry in motion happened. Something, perhaps my limbic angel, told me that underneath his ominous dark side, he was terrified, and that is what gave me the courage to walk into his Hell.

Here Sam describes a more recent session:

> "I told you I was really scared of turning into Satan and was terrified. You held my hand and I wept. You asked me how I wanted to work and I found myself kneeling with my head on your mattress with lots of tears and snot flowing, as if I was bowing down before God as a hopeless damned soul. You noted my sense of 'heaviness', of having to hold myself, and you, sitting beside me, supported the weight of the head and upper torso, and then my whole weight (200lb) with me across your torso as I wept. I was conscious of holding onto your arms and feeling the flesh of your arm, as if feeling real flesh for the very first time. You then suggested I find the middle human position, of kneeling and simply asking for forgiveness instead of the (my) grandiose defenses of omnipotent God and Satan."

The alchemy of touch was happening on many levels. (As our eyes met, I sensed the wounded human soul behind Sam's 'evil eye' and he saw in me a safe enough mix of darkness and light to trust that he could share some of the evilness in his eye.) Grace of self is not easily unveiled, but it helps when we can glimpse the desperate human being who is veiled behind our demons. Something like this was set in motion for Sam as he received my touch. As he puts it:

> "The essence of our work ... was the holding together of two things: the absolute simplicity of being gently, physically touched/held and the creation of a momentary space in which you made the very quiet suggestion to me (when faced with my fiery demon) that I allow the alchemy of the defenses to work."

So I did two things. I physically touched Sam and I invited him to think and move closer – as I had in our first encounter – closer to the angel in his demon. Anchored in our simple human contact, he was able to grasp that his angel-turned-demon had originally come to him with the same humanity that I had embodied in my touch. In his case, however, because of the specific culture and metaphor from which he came, and in response to his mother's profound rejection of her own and his life force, Sam's angel had pulled him up or perhaps down into a Heaven and Hell cosmology and become its demonic guardian. The angel had become the demonic guardian. In Sam's words:

> "In my ordination as a priest, I had turned down life (offered up my very self-hood and sexuality in the form of a cross), and now I was opening upwards to life, and in physical touch with your flesh to affirm it. I felt able to breathe very deeply, and felt like a 'very old soul' from the Mountains of Lebanon where the splitting-belief in God and Evil Eye were very strong – but now the alchemy was working ... I kept my hands on your face, arms and hands, feeling your flesh and the realness and poetry of the contact ... I felt, as if for the first time, what it was like to be a human being in real time and space."

The body's language is poetry because it brings the unity that existed before there were words. Sam was graced in being able to begin a simple human dialogue with his fiery friend-foe-friend. And now I finally give

101

you the secret of unveiling the grace of self ... take your demons to lunch!

## References

Berry, W. (1999) The Real Work, The Selected Poems of Wendell Berry, Counterpoint

Blake, W. (1988) Songs of Innocence. The Complete Poetry and Prose of William Blake. Random House (Anchor Books), New York, pp. 7–17.

Coelho, P (1998) Part II. The Alchemist. Harper Collins, New York, pp. 51–163.

Edinger, E. (1986) The Bible and the Psyche, Toronto: Inner City Books. (Story reported by Edward Edinger in the course of his audio-taped lecture series on the Old Testament at the Los Angeles Jung Institute. The story apparently originated with the New York analyst Esther Harding who knew the person in England to whom it happened.)

Kalshed, D. (1996) Further Clinical Illustrations of the Self-Care System. The Inner World of Trauma. Routledge, London, pp. 41–67.

Koch, K (May 14, 1998) preview of an article by Kenneth Koch from the New York Review of Books, volume 45, number 8.

Kurosawa, A. (1983) Something like an Autobiography. (A. E. Bock, Trans.). Vintage Books, New York.

Milton, J. (1998) John Milton the Complete Poems. Sonnet XVI ("On His Blindness"). Penguin Books (Classics), London, p. 84.

Reich, W. (1976- published by Farrar, Straus in 1966) The Genital Embrace from the book, The Murder of Christ. Pocket Books, New York, pp. 35–43

Shakespeare, W. (1988) The Arden Shakespeare (Thompson Learning). The Merchant of Venice. Act IV, Scene 1. (Portia's Soliloquy). Thompson Learning, London, pp. 103–122.

Yeats, W. B. (1996) The Collected Poems of W. B. Yeats. Among School Children – a Meditation on Life. Simon & Schuster, Inc., New York, pp. 215–217.

## About the Author

Robert Lewis, M. D., in private practice in New York, is a senior trainer on the IIBA faculty, and a member of the clinical faculty of the NYU/Mount Sinai Medical Center. He has published extensively on the integration of early developmental and relational issues into the basic bioenergetic approach. Bob has long been interested in the sensory-motor story which trauma engraves in our bodies. He coined the term "cephalic shock" to capture the psychosomatic experience of what Winnicott called the mind as the locus of the false self. His elucidation of Cephalic Shock and way of working with the head, voice, and dia-phragmatic connections to the pelvis, are beyond words. He has found the Attachment paradigm deeply confirming of the centrality of rela-tionship in his clinical approach. Bob aims for and is touched by the moments of encounter in which implicit mystery becomes almost pal-pable. He leads workshops in Europe and the Americas, and residential intensives on Long Island, New York.

docboblewis@gmail.com
bodymindcentral.com

# Introduction to Creative Writing Section

Dear Reader,

The previous article was on the poetry of the body. It included poetry as well as the fluid prose of Bob Lewis. This theme of poetry in the body inspired my idea to include some creative writing in this volume of the IIBA journal. I requested some creative writing pieces and these two were selected. I hope you enjoy the rich poetry on various subjects by Linda Neal and some grief poetry that I wrote a few years ago.

Traditionally, this journal has been for scientific or clinical material. However, the muse of writing fiction (or truth) in forms less tied to science exists in many of us. It may be an avenue for healing or a form to express ones passion, joy, or pleasure. Bioenergetics seeks to help us expand our horizons. These creative expressions are one avenue into this expansion beyond our usual boundaries.

*Vincentia Schroeter*

# Poems

*Linda Neal*

## A Thunder of Swans

Forget about masks. Forget about cracked eggs
on your mother's kitchen floor. Forget about fear.
Live in the wild elements, no matter how hostile they seem.

Be the woman who cries out in the open field
the man who carries his losses on his lips.
Be a crack of thunder. Re-member yourself.
    Become both expert and novice,
    speaking the eloquent language
    of body, full as a summer-red grape
    fleshing into the sky, because
    you are riding this horse of your life
    all the way to the end.

Forget about appearance and disappearance. Forget everything
you ever learned about being small
because the ride offers inevitable gifts. Fighting against the end,
even against the earth's melting at its poles,
is a grand waste of time. So flow toward unknown dimensions
toward an immense energy field of loss and abundance

Where there are no questions and no answers
only weeping and laughter, laughter and weeping
the sole anodynes in the end. So fly
like a thunder of swans. Shake and shimmer
in the excruciating joy
of your exquisitely bearable, temporary life.

## CLOUD LIFE

I am here
on a temporary assignment
that I keep trying
to make permanent
while clouds

    float
in a blue sky
    changing their shape
    forming
and reforming.
I never expected
to be like a cloud
    myself

    skinny
then full
then
      gone

## MARY OLIVER

She walks with a stick
not for support, but to point
toward the poems
that live in trees and dunes
along the Cape Cod Shore.

She wends her way
down the post office steps
and along the narrow streets
of Provincetown
weaving magic with her pen.

While Summer visits
other lands
of palms and geckos
where painters paint
and the rain is soft.

This new pied piper
of the faded jeans
and Patagonia pullover
can lead you and your child
straight to the center
of Spring.

A soft breeze and a strong wind
she's pointing her wand
at Winter's dappled light
the grey sky
and the mythological bear
that lives in the woods nearby.

## MOTHER TO A MAN

As he curls into the couch
lounging, listening
to loud music
I don't understand
he becomes a lump
deep inside of me
stone cold
because
I am incapable
of knowing him, I mean
understanding
    the young hairs on his chest
    or the brown of his eyes
    that hang over him
    like a trench coat.
I wonder if he senses
my desire to get close
rub him with rose petals and talcum
wash orange-scented shampoo into his hair
like I used to
when he dodges past me
naked on his way to the shower

The distance between us mounts
even as he stands
in my kitchen
or goes far away, gazing at coals
in the fireplace
even further in his bedroom
sleeping
    between flannel sheets
    dreaming of the hands
    of another woman
    future mother of his son.

## TOWARD WATER

On this cold November morning
I sit at the window, with my hot coffee
looking out at the nearby pine,
its branches spread out against the sky
its cones hanging on by the hundreds.
One thuds to the damp morning ground.
A squirrel cracks another in her jaw
but our destinies do not intertwine
even though when I was eight I shinnied
up bark in old jeans. The season didn't matter.

Truth about myself or time
came down to
the classroom of my childhood
where a Mason jar stood on an oak table
in the corner
and inside an embryo
floated
delivered into water
dead

and the contraction
in the pit of my stomach
when my mother walked into a room
then my expansion in rain
sloshing through puddles
alongside bones and coins
in my red rubber boots.

Trees and water
were my hedges against
my parents' dark weather
the muddy confluence of family strife,
so at night in the dark

the merging of the one with the many
the small with the large.
Some nights I became so small
I could hide inside a drop of water
and becoming water
be the whole ocean,
be everywhere at once
see my grandmother's grandmother
washing her black hair in a lake
and myself, safe and small
inside my mother,
before I entered the plains
of daughterhood and danger.

Safe in salty water,
alone and becoming, unseen unborn,
I could thrum a string
for the one who was to learn
no safety, not even, especially not
in the net of family.
Fished out of my warm and private sea
thrown up on dry land
I have looked for water
wherever I go, and exposed
to darker energies of close kin
I trek down
to damp sand, swim in the sea
search for wet valleys
sit at the mouths of caves
and the edges of waterfalls
exploring the flooded wilderness
of my life
absorbing the pulse of water
to learn life not as a maze but a labyrinth.

## ABOUT THE AUTHOR

Linda Neal has been a marriage, family therapist for twenty-five years. She lives, works, writes, gardens, walks on the beach, leads support groups at the Cancer Support Community and teaches meditation in Redondo Beach, CA. She completed the bioenergetic training program in 2004.

Linda Neal
1110 Ynez Avenue
Redondo Beach, Ca 90277
310-316-9931
lindaneal@dslextreme.com

# GRIEVING MOM POEMS

*Vincentia Schroeter*

The following are some poems I wrote to help me cope with the death of my mother. <u>Living with an Empty Chair</u> is a book on grief by Dr. Roberta Temes[1]. Temes states that the stages of grief are Numbness, Disorganization, and finally, Reorganization. In the Numbness stage, one is in a hazy state in body and mind. This normal state helps protect us from the enormity of our grief. In the stage of Disorganization, the haze begins to lift as the full meaning of our loss is felt. It is normal in this stage to feel the vacuum of acute loneliness and emptiness. During the Reorganization stage, we begin to re-invest in the future. We gradually displace some of the emotional investment we had in the deceased. It is normal to displace some of that emotion toward other people and things.

Although these stages are universal, Temes makes the point that grief is as individual as those of us who feel it and as varied as the circumstances of death which occurs. These poems are my individual expression and the circumstance was the death of my mother, who died after a long and well-lived life. The poems are divided by the stages of grief stated above.

---

1 Temes, Roberta, (1991), Living with an Empty Chair, a guide through grief.(New Horizon Press, Far Hills, NJ)

## (GRIEF STAGE 1: NUMBNESS)

### MAMAGONE

Time to stare out over a vast sky.
Watch ocean waves ebb and flow me into space,
Let a hot wind warm me,
A cold drink cool me.

I want only to be passive and still.
My body wants to rest.
My mind wants to float.

But the world pulls me back
When I just want to sink
Into my husband's arms,
 A big stuffed chair,
 A cozy warm bed.

I stare at a smiling puffy lamb I had given her.
His arms encircle a purple teddy bear whose shirt reads,
"Love you, Mother" …

It is unreal that you are gone.

*8-8-2006*

## MAMAGONE 2

They took her away.
We all arrived
One by one, family by family falling into
Fears, tears, hugs.

Slow motion, everyone pausing at her empty bed,
Reverent.
One sister touches and smells her pillow and sheets,
While I sit frozen in a chair, clutching a pillow,
Watching.

In other rooms, they plan her funeral,
Cleaning, eating, preparing words to honor her.

On the periphery of stunned adults in startled grief,
        Kids run through the house and around the summer yard:
        Jump off the roof,
        Chase each other with water balloons,
        Dart around corners, surefooted,
        Laughing, bonding with cousins,
        Oblivious.
                One day,
                They'll become adults
                And slow in the wake of the death of their parent.
Everything changes.
The worn, smooth, familiar stones beneath me,
Once sure in their support of my every step,
Are loose,
Making me slip and walk gingerly,
Surprising my feet, who don't seem to know:
She was my ground.

*8-26-2006*

## (Grief Stage 2: Disorganization)

### Beneath the Reunion Planning

Doing is Being.
Keeping us alive since Mom died.
Everybody planning details for a reunion:
Site, decorations, evites, and food.

Then my brother sends an email ending in capital letters,
"I MISS MY MOMMY".
Doing stops in its tracks.
I blink and stare at those words as my eyes water.
I pause in my feverish planning of a family reunion
To understand its urgent purpose:

Just hands grabbing other hands
To pull us up into life
When gravity pulls us down
To hover at our mother's grave.

I drag around my bucket full of tears,
Ignore its weight,
Pulling myself through these days.

My eyes squint because the sun is too bright right now.
I feel drawn to night.
In the cool of the dark sky,
I could stare forever at stars.
Night stars know more about the mysteries of heaven and the afterlife
than these forced sunny smiles of daytime doings and actions all covering for truth best revealed to me at night:
I am in deep sorrow.
Night slows the day and invites me to pause and breathe more truth:
To be sad, to cry, to hurt, to feel a little scared of dying myself.

The bucket fills with tears, I succumb to the heaviness of its weight,
Stop and pour it out into the welcome blackness of night.

Life seems shorter, more real in its shortness, since Mom died.

Dad just lost his best friend after sixty years of marriage.
What does he reach for to get through the day?
Does he grab for a hand?
Flesh he can still touch in life, which belongs to those he has left?
He visits, he calls,
He helps plan a reunion for a sunny day next Spring.

*11-13-2006*

## SIBLING POEM

A leaf drops into the river.
I watch until it disappears from sight.
I want to float away myself.

I see you on the nearby shore.
I hear you sobbing.
I hold you as you cry.
I feel the hot rush of my tears.
You hold me while I cry.

Our hearts are breaking in the same place,
The place reserved for mother love,
Where the one who carried us into life
Has gone and left us here alone.

If not for the mirror we become for each other
I think I could break.

I feel the gritty pebbles of sandy shore beneath my bare feet.
We walk together in this tenuous land between life and death.

*12-11-2006*

## (Stage 3: Reorganization)

### Las Flores Blancas

I wake up cringing on the first day of Spring.
Today is Mom's first birthday since she died last summer.

I walk downstairs feeling fragile.
A profusion of new white flowers dot the dark green bushes that climb
the walls outside my kitchen windows.
Startled, I gasp at this beautiful greeting from nature.

My eyes fill with the slow undulations of white petals.
I sense a confident smiling power above me,
Like when Glinda, the Good Witch, looks down from the sky, circles
her wand and wakens Dorothy from her drugged sleep.

Once on her birthday Mom proudly told me, "I bring the Spring."
She opened a hundred white flowers in my garden today.
I feel her faith-filled, hope-filled presence drawing me to look closely
at these flowers:
Each shaped like gently cupped hands,
Swaying slowly in the warm breeze.

They beckon me to climb inside.
I crawl inside their lap,
They rock me until my pain subsides,

Creating room for hope and love,
As nature insists with buds that burst through each new Spring,
No matter how harsh Winter has been.

*3-21-2007*

## ABOUT THE AUTHOR

Vincentia Schroeter has kept personal journals since she was fifteen. She likes to both draw and write in these journals. Working through painful issues has often involved some creative writing. In her psychotherapy practice, one of her specialities is working with grief. Workshops on grief have included some of the poems that are included here. Her website is vincentiaschroeterphd.com.

Vincentia Schroeter
P. O. Box 235738
Encinitas, California
92023
U. S. A.

# Book Reviews

## Epigenetics and Body Psychotherapy

*Margit Koemeda-Lutz*

Prof. Dr.med. Joachim Bauer from the University of Freiburg in Germany will be one of our key note speakers at the next International Conference of the IIBA, October 26th–30th in San Diego, California.

There are two books which impressed me as extremely valuable for body psychotherapists and which made me suggest his invitation to our next conference.

"Das Gedächtnis des Körpers – Wie Beziehungen und Lebensstile unsere Gene steuern" (The Memory of the Body – how relationships and life styles regulate our genes; transl. M. K.) was first published in 2002.

In his first chapters Bauer explains the structure and function of DNS sequences in each of our cells, of gene transcription and protein synthesis, in a way that readers not familiar with microbiological knowledge easily grasp some of the major principles of current genetic knowledge.

New to me, whose neurobiological and neuropsychological education dates back to the 1970s, was, that Mendel's laws of heredity explain only a very small proportion of phenotypic variation, i. e., there exist very few genes that get active, mostly insensitive to environmental conditions (like the ones that determine the colour of our eyes, or illnesses as Chorea Huntington, hemophilia etc.).

Human beings share the same genetic blueprints to the incredible degree of 99.9%! The obvious variation between individuals therefore is due to the interaction between environmental (including cellular and proprioceptive) signals and genes.

Joachim Bauer is a medical doctor, specializing in internal and psychosomatic medicine and psychiatry. In addition he is a psychotherapist. He has done research in molecular biology and is, since 1992, professor for psychoneuroimmunology at the University of Freiburg in Germany.

He successfully conveys his vast knowledge to a wider public interested in questions of psychosomatic health and illness. He has frequently been an appreciated guest in scientifically oriented talk shows on TV and a valued keynote speaker at many scientific conferences.

Bauer reviews and reflects on an immense body of microbiological, psychiatric and psychosomatic research literature to propose a quite coherent model of how life experiences, especially early in life, interact with the genetically designed human potential in order to shape individual personalities on different – mental, emotional, behavioural, physiological and morphological – levels.

He demonstrates that – more than anything – interpersonal relationships influence somatic processes. This influence reaches as "deep" as to the regulation of gene activity. It is effective in adult human beings, and even more so during infancy and prenatal development.

As psychotherapists we know that early experiences shape feeling, thinking and behavioural patterns. Bauer reviews several empirical studies, which prove that they also shape our somatic functioning, such as physiological patterns and the neuronal architecture in our brains (p 195). Attuned positive bonding in early childhood protects stress genes from over-reactivity in later life. Our brain "translates" sensory input into biological signals. Positive human relationships constitute the best "medication without side effects" for coping with psychic and somatic stress.

Early in life neuronal networks develop that later determine how a person appraises his or her environment and how he/she copes with challenging events in his/her life. The "construction" of neuronal networks (morphology/architecture and functional patterns) depends on early (relational) experiences. If they are positive, they foster resilience, if they are detrimental (like e. g. neglect, abuse, violence), they may lead to dissociative patterns and contribute as etiological factors to the evolution of psychiatric disorders. Each of our experiences is stored in neuronal networks and changes their microstructure, which results in a life long plasticity of the brain (p. 90).

All mental operations are facilitated by the interconnections of nerve cell assemblies (p. 72). Perceptions and notions are based on synaptic connections between nerve cells, forming networks, which by this establish representations of perceptions and notions.

Synapses are involved in exchanging information, which activate specific genes in these nerve cells. In this way active synapses enhance their structure, while inactive synapses dissolve: "Use it or loose it". Frequent and intense experiences strengthen and enhance the interconnection of cell assemblies and networks. Simultaneous, synchronic, rhythmical bioelectric activities (ca. 40 Hz) in cells create networks. "Cells that fire together, wire together".

This happens by activation of nerve cell growth genes like BNDF (brain derived neurotrophic factor), CNTF (ciliary neurotrophic factor), NGF (nerve growth factor) etc. (p. 80). Neurotransmitters activate genes that cause protein production and by this a strengthening of receptors.

With the Human Genome Project, which was accomplished in 2000, the totality of all human genes – comprising about 3.9 billions of nucleotides – was decoded. Genetic "texts", i.e. DNS sequences, are fixed for each organism and subject to hereditary processes. The "expression" and activity of most genes though is subject to regulation in interaction with "contextual" (cells and other organs, proprioception) and environmental stimuli and is a life long "task". Individual experiences provoke and form reaction patterns that influence this regulation.

Only 1–2% of all human diseases are caused by gene mutations.

Certain substances or environmental factors (transcription factors, UV light, nutritional factors, perceived relational situations) absorb or activate promoters, i.e. regulatory sequences on specific genes.

## STRESS

Most perceptions are processed unconsciously in human organisms. Our nervous system initiates or triggers many psychic and somatic reactions without our awareness.

Stress in so-called civilized societies is mainly caused by interpersonal conflicts and lack of social support, as when needs and desires are not communicated, or by offenses, hurt and humiliation.

As clinicians we are familiar with the Hypothalamus-pituitary and adrenal gland-stress axis and its regulatory functions in cortisol synthesis and release. But that this stress system is individually coined (conditioned) in every single organism may not have been so widely known. In addition to heightened (raised) cortisol levels, stress also causes the release of other transmitters noxious to nerve cells, e. g. adrenaline, noradrenalin and glutamate (p. 74). Increased cortisol and glutamate concentrations in the brain can cause cell decline, especially in the hippocampus, responsible for memory functions (p. 50).

Cortisol has lasting effects on the immune system, blocks interleukins and tumor necrosis factor. These immunological transmitters are no longer produced in sufficient quantities, because cortisol blocks all genes responsible for their production.

Stress increases the susceptibility for virus infections. Cortisol represses fever and other important defence reactions necessary for healing (p. 49).

Stress can have negative effects on the course of several diseases: multiple sclerosis, rheumatoid arthritis, skin diseases (like psoriasis), diabetes, coronary and heart conditions.

According to Bauer, relationships are biologically based factors of health. When interpersonal relationships decrease quantitatively and qualitatively, health disorders increase (p. 19).

In addition to these more basic principles of interactions between individual organisms and environmental factors, Bauer delineates neurobiologically and interpersonally based etiological models on some of the most prevalent illnesses in Western societies: depression, coronary and heart diseases, cancer, pain syndromes, post traumatic stress disorders and burnout states.

**Depression:** Life events not only influence the well-being of a person, but substantially dysregulate gene activity and other somatic processes, resulting e. g. in sleep disorders, lack of motivation and agitation. With repeated depressive episodes there need not be any triggering events for a new episode any more. Depression is biologically conditioned. Depression is an over activation of the stress system. It has been demonstrated that depressive patients have significantly more problems and losses in their early relationships as compared to non-depressive controls.

**Coronary and Heart Diseases:** Several studies have shown the relationship between stress and depression and their influence on coronary and heart diseases. A combination of heart condition and depression bears a triple risk of mortality. Depression decreases heart rate variability and therefore increases the risk of heart diseases.

**Cancer:** Stress and depression also influence the immunological defence and risk of tumor growth. Increased cortisol levels block immunological and inflammatory responses (reduction of natural killer cells). Psychotherapeutic support reduces the risk of mortality.

**Pain syndromes:** Pain experiences leave imprints in our neuronal system like any other experiences, namely in the sensory area of the cortex and in the gyrus cinguli, and facilitate future sensations of pain. Psychological and somatic pains "use" the same brain structures. Therefore psychological support and relaxation decrease the probability of pain sensations.

**Post traumatic stress disorder (PTSD):** In traumatic situations dissociation serves as a protective mechanism as genes for the production of endorphins are activated. The alarm reaction is stored in the amygdala and the person develops a chronic amygdaloid over activity and exhibits an increased sensitization towards stress. This is the starting point for dissociative disorders, borderline personality or eating disorders to evolve.

Summarizing, Bauer reviews several studies that demonstrate that psychotherapy is a method of healing which influences psyche and body at the same time.

## MIRROR NEURONS AND BODY PSYCHOTHERAPY

### Margit Koemeda-Lutz

The second book by Bauer that fascinated me was "Warum ich fühle, was du fühlst – Intuitive Kommunikation und das Geheimnis der Spiegelneurone" (Why I feel what you feel – intuitive communication and the mystery of mirror neurons; transl. M.K.). It was published in 2005.

It answers questions like, why do we intuitively understand what others feel and why can we empathize with others' joys and sorrows?

Bauer elaborates on the far reaching consequences of Rizzolatti's and coworker's discovery of the mirror neurons in the premotor area of the cortex (1996, 2001, 2002, 2003) One of the decisive starting points was the observation that people unconsciously react to gestures and imitate facial expressions while in communication with each other. They also focus their attention on the same objects (joint attention). Moods, feelings and body postures seem to be contagious. Moreover, when we observe another person we can to a certain degree intuitively predict some of his/her consecutive actions, an ability which can be life saving in dangerous situations. From a glance at another person we can tell his/her feelings, wishes and intentions.

Action plans are represented in the premotor area of the cortex. Here, evoked potentials can be traced, 100–200 ms before motor neurons that innervate our muscles actually fire.

Bauer reports on the experiments that Rizzolatti et al. conducted to find out that action plans are represented in these premotor areas of our brains. These experiments also demonstrated that these same neurons also fired when a monkey only watched another monkey execute one such action (e. g. grasped a coconut). This proved that resonance does have a neurobiological basis. Mirror neurons involuntarily simulate what others do while we watch them (including the subjective perspective of what this feels like).

Sometimes the observation of only a fragment of a whole action pattern is sufficient to convey an anticipation of what the other person is about to do (p. 31 Umiltá et al. 2001). This is not only true for actions but also for feeling and thinking patterns.

Intuition needs to be supplemented by rational analysis (which is slow). Fear, stress and tension significantly reduce the signal ratio of our mirror neurons.

By observing others we acquire potential action patterns (software for action). If compatible motivations are added, a person will act.

From our third year in life till about 16 years inhibiting factors prevent individuals to imitate everything they observe. But resonating mirror neurons increase the readiness to act.

Behavior is connected to needs. While planning motor behaviour, humans most of the time try to anticipate the consequences of such behaviour. Proprioceptive simulations help with this by furnishing input to the sensoric cortex.

In the inferior parietal cortex we generate sensoric images. In the insula, general body sensations, especially of our inner organs (e.g. feelings of disgust) are represented. Mirror neurons in the Gyrus Cinguli are nerve cells for empathy and compassion (p. 49).

On the basis of such neuroscientific findings, Bauer delineates a functional model for empathy: 1) The primary visual cortex is part of the occipital lobe; starting from this area optical impressions are composed to perceived pictures; 2) In the Sulcus temporalis inferior (STS) which is part of the temporal lobe, behaviour of an observed person is interpreted; 3) the premotor cortex in the frontal lobe contains representations of complex behavioural motor patterns and 4) the inferior part of the parietal lobe contains representations of how it feels to behave as planned in 3). **Mirror neurons have been found in 2), 3) and 4).**

Mirror neurons use neurobiological mechanisms of the observer to simulate what happens in the observed person. They are the neurobiological basis for intuitive, spontaneous comprehension and the basis of what we call the Theory of Mind (TOM).

The right hemisphere stores sensations that belong to and are to be expected in interpersonal situations. As soon as the person becomes active the LH also gets activated.

Mirror neurons are the neuronal basis of a superindividual, intuitively accessible, shared realm of comprehension (p. 106).

Social attention and attunement increases the release of neurotransmitters and hormones (opiods, dopamine, oxytocin). Receiving a minimum of resonance is a crucial biological need.

Infants exposed to long lasting deficits in caregiving and attunement will exhibit an increased sensitivity in their stress genes (p. 107).

Empathy is learned behaviour (i. e. it is a skill that requires training). And there is healing power in mirroring and empathic reactions by therapists to the patients' narratives about trauma, neglect or abuse.

Unfortunately, Bauer (see pp. 140ff.) does not seem to know much about body psychotherapeutic modalities. Maybe a new and fermenting dialogue can begin at the San Diego conference in 2011.

## MARGIT KOEMEDA-LUTZ: "INTELLIGENTE EMOTIONALITÄT" (INTELLIGENT EMOTIONALITY)

### Angela Klopstech

For a number of years, I have made the case that the viability of Bio-energetic Analysis – definitely in the sense of survival but also in the sense of thriving – will require that it more fully attempts to enter the mainstream with its attendant opportunities and dangers, albeit without loosing its roots and core. Among other things, this means re-evaluation of old and integration of new concepts. It particularly means casting a curious eye on the research from contemporary neuroscience and its effect on the understanding of the world of human emotions while maintaining the essence of the bioenergetic understanding of emotions. In her recently published book "Intelligente Emotionalität", which is not primarily intended for professionals, but for a broad readership, Margit Koemeda, the past editor and current co-editor of this journal, straddles this divide gracefully and competently. Unfortunately, at this point in time, the book is only available in German. The appropriate English translation would be "Intelligent Emotionality", and it can only be hoped that an English translation will be on the market soon.

Margit Koemeda is known within the bioenergetic community as a faculty member, board member of the scientific committee, and as a writer and editor. In her home country of Switzerland, beyond the boundaries of her own bioenergetic society, she is intensely involved in the broader scientific and political world of psychotherapy, again as a writer and in various organizational functions. Her book is both a testimony to and a result of her wide-spanning knowledge, interests and involvements.

This book is about emotions and the role they play in our lives, or in contemporary professional terms, about emotions and their regulation. The underlying notion is that emotions, while they are not the exclusive determinant of our thinking and behavior, "if correctly perceived, carefully attuned, regularly 'cleansed', well regulated and intelligently communicated, can become a valuable energy source for your everyday behavior and thinking" (p. 13). Throughout the book Koemeda explains what this means as she describes with many examples how it can be attempted and, hopefully, achieved. True to her bioenergetic background, and her (I assume) personal belief, the author makes it her agenda to show how important it is to give emotions more space in our lives.

The book is divided into two sections, 'Basics' and '(clinical) Applications', and contains a 'checklist for emotional health' as an appendix. This main body of the book is preceded by an introduction that is a true introduction in the sense that it sets the stage and emotional tone for the book, rather than just giving a list of the following chapters together with an explanatory sentence.

The first part of the book deals with basic questions such as: what are emotions; how are they embedded in and related to cultural context; which role they play in communication and social interaction; and how they develop over the life span. The elaborations on these topics are substantiated and greatly enhanced by an excursion into the field of neuropsychology and neurobiology. The author's overview of the relevant neuroscience is easily understandable yet theoretically sound.

This is what makes this part of the book stand out in a book market which has recently been flooded with publications on the brain/behavior connection: its immense readability despite not sacrificing and not skimping on slow-to-read theory that provides necessary background knowledge of brain structures, systems and processes.

The first section concludes with case vignettes focusing on specific examples of how intrapsychic regulation of emotions (regulation within the person) and interpsychic regulation (regulation through and with another person) might be worked at and worked out within the therapeutic relationship.

The second part explores four realms of emotion in more depth: grief and depression, anger and rage, fear and anxiety, lust and love. Using examples from her clinical practice, Koemeda outlines different paths of self regulation within these arenas of emotion. She skillfully imports basic bioenergetic principles, e.g. emphasizing the regulatory function of the expression and or/discharge of anger, without ever talking about Bioenergetics explicitly. I enjoyed particularly the lighthearted chapter on 'lust and love', where the author gets down deep into the complications and vicissitudes of the arguably most complex emotion, while keeping an easy touch. In her last chapter she draws careful conclusions between malfunctioning emotional regulation and malfunctioning physical regulations, commonly called diseases.

Throughout her book, Koemeda uses many and various examples, either from her practice as a psychotherapist or at times from literature. Every idea is illuminated by a case vignette or a concrete description. Koemeda's use of language and writing style are a successful blend of the metaphorical and the concrete, and dovetail nicely with her purpose of demonstrating that "emotions give 'color' to our experiences, our behaviors, our communications" (p. 10).

Both content and writing style make the book not only a pleasure to read but also into a good read across the board. Though obviously intended for the general public, it is certainly of interest for the bioenergetically informed reader and anyone who is interested in what psychologists call emotion and emotional regulation.

What makes the book of particular value for bioenergetic therapists is the fact that the therapy vignettes invariably make apparent the underlying bioenergetic thinking, even though interventions are not labeled as such. It may help us as bioenergetic therapists with our identity and self definition. By knowing that we do not have to 'do' heavy-handed bioenergetics in order to do bioenergetic therapy, we can take it for granted that we fit in.

ABOUT THE AUTHOR

Angela Klopstech, PhD, Dipl.-Psych.,
40–50 East Tenth Street, #1c
New York, NY 10003
212-260-3289
klopkoltuv@aol.com

## DANIEL SIEGEL: MINDSIGHT

*Robert Hilton*

When I first heard Daniel Siegel speak in 1999, I thought to myself, this man explains the neurological basis for the work we do as somatic therapists. My response was to his discussion of his first book, *The Developing Mind*. He has since written three other books: *The Mindful Brain*, *Mindsight* and *The Mindful Therapist*. This review is limited to *Mindsight*. You can go to Google on your computer and type in Mindsight and find many critical reviews of this book. I have chosen to write a review with my audience in mind. While giving you a taste of the overall message of the book I have deliberately focused on the parts that are particularly relevant to us as somatic psychotherapists.

Siegel defines mindsight as follows, "Mindsight is a process that enables us to modify the flow of energy and information within a Triangle of Well-Being. The *monitoring* aspect of mindsight involves sensing this flow within ourselves – perceiving it in our own nervous systems, which we are calling Brain – and within others through our Relationships, which involve the sharing of energy and information flow through various means of communication. We then can *modify* this flow through awareness and intention, fundamental aspects of our mind, directly shaping the paths that energy and information flow take in our lives."

The illustration he likes to use in the book regarding mindsight, or the monitoring and modifying of the flow of energy, is that of a bicycle wheel where you have a hub in the center, a rim on the outside and spokes that go from the hub to the rim. The hub becomes the inner place of the mind from which we become aware. The spokes represent how we direct our attention to a particular part of the rim. The hub can be seen as a visual metaphor for our prefrontal cortex. At any one time you may be able to direct your attention to various feelings and actions that are on the rim. As you do that you begin to realize that you are not defined by these experiences, that there is a you in the hub who can make decisions about where to focus your attention. Siegel says, "The hub of our mind is always available to us, right now. And it's from this hub that we enter a compassionate state of connection to ourselves, and feel compassion for others."

Anything that may come into our awareness may be one of the points on the rim. One sector on the rim is our inward sense of the body, the sensations in our limbs and our facial muscles, the feelings in the organs of our torso - our lungs, our heart, and our intestines. All of the body brings its wisdom up into our mind, and this bodily sense we can bring into our awareness. By doing a simple exercise of following our breath we are able to expand our awareness and thus our hub of awareness expands. Siegel in referring to a patient whom he had taught to follow his breath in this way says, "There is a place deep within us that is observant, objective, and open. This is the receptive hub of the mind, the tranquil depth of the mental sea." He goes on to say that from this depth his patient, "could use the power of reflective awareness to alter the way his brain functioned and ultimately to change the structure of his brain." In another place he states simply,

"One of the key practical lessons of modern neuroscience is that the power to direct our attention has within it the power to shape our brain's firing patterns, as well as the power to shape the architecture".

Bodily regulation, attuned communication, emotional balance, response flexibility, fear modulation, empathy, insight, moral awareness and intuition are a list of some of the elements of emotional well being and they all have a prefrontal function in the brain. Intuition, for example can be seen as how the middle prefrontal cortex gives us access to the wisdom of the body. This region receives information from throughout the interior of the body, including the viscera – such as our heart and intestines-and uses this input to give us a "heart sense" of what to do or a "gut feeling" about the right choice. Siegel states, "This integrative function illuminates how reasoning, once thought to be a "purely logical" mode of thinking, is in fact dependent on the non-rational processing of our bodies. Such intuition helps us make wise decisions, not just logical ones."

One chapter with particular relevance for us as somatic therapists is entitled, "Cut Off From The Neck Down: *Reconnecting the Mind and the Body*." He describes a case with a patient. The patient as a result of childhood trauma had decided not to feel anything again. She demonstrated this comment by using her finger like a knife and cutting off her head. Yet she had heart palpitations and stated, "I guess there has to be something more to life than just this." Siegel's description of this patient sounds like a somatic therapist talking. He reports the following: "Halfway through Anne's second visit, a quotation from James Joyce that I'd heard somewhere popped into my head: Mr. Duffy 'lived at a little distance from his body.' It was in the way she moved, the stiffness of her gait, the way she held her hands motionless in her lap. (Her throat cutting gesture stood out even more in retrospect.) It was also emerging from her account of a limited, rigid inner life lived only above the shoulders."

He goes on to describe exactly what happens in our brain when we decide not to feel anything again. He also describes exercises that help in the recovery of the brain's capacity to receive previously frightening information. The key, of course, to all of this is the empathic attunement of the therapist. He describes how in the beginning of the therapy with this patient he did a body scan. When she came to her chest where all the sadness had been hidden she began to hyperventilate and panic. He brought her back from the panic and suggested exercises she could do at home to help her. In a later session he returned to the body scan and this time when she contacted her chest she began to feel heaviness and tightness in her throat. Tears filled her eyes and she felt a profound sense of sadness. At first Siegel says her tears were slow, a few drops, then when she noticed them she wiped them away. Then he states, "As we stayed together with whatever she was feeling, she began to sob uncontrollably, her body bent over as she moaned in pain. I let her sense our connection with my own non-verbal signals - a sigh, a quiet "ummmm", the rhythm of our breathing in synch. When she opened her eyes and we looked at each other, I noticed my own tears."

In a session with Stuart, a different client, Siegel recalls reminding the client of an event that he had told him about that happened in the client's childhood. The man was deeply moved and replied with tears, "I can't believe you remembered what I said months ago...I can't believe you really know me." Siegel writes, "I can't really put words to what happened, but – half a year into therapy – there now seemed to be a "we" in the room. If we had had brain monitors on hand, I think they would have picked up the resonance between us. Just as Stuart had been moved to tears at realizing that his mind was in mine, I felt deeply moved by feeling, for the first time, that mine was in his. There was a deep and open connection between us."

In summary, this book provides a clear description of the function of the mind and brain in psychotherapy and suggests ways that through mindfulness and attention we can actually change our brain's structure. Siegel believes that through this process we can become our own best friend and form a connection that is like that of a secure attachment. He also demonstrates the importance of the body and a deep empathic attunement in this process. It is quite heartening to read this coming from one of the leaders in the field of neurobiology and mindfulness meditation. I highly recommend this book to any therapist.

Daniel Siegel will be one of the guest speakers at our IIBA conference in October, 2011. After his presentation, Louise Frechette will offer a video presentation demonstrating her bioenergetic work with a client. Following the video presentation I will interview Siegel regarding his work and how it relates to what we do as somatic therapists. The following are some of the questions I will be discussing with him:

How do we integrate mindfulness meditation and the healthy function of the brain with the body and relationship?

Can a secure attachment be established in the brain through mindfulness meditation alone?

How important is the therapeutic relationship in securing or maintaining affect regulation in the client?

Can mindfulness exercises and/or the relationship with the therapist create a healthy brain state and thereby bypass the early traumas that are embedded in the body?

How differently do we work with clients who have very little or no access to a basic self or safe place for refuge?

(I would welcome any further questions you might have that I could present in the interview. You can reach me at rhilton@cox.net.)

## ABOUT THE AUTHOR

Robert Hilton, PhD, has attained IIBA Emeritus Faculty status. An internationally celebrated trainer, he is the author of *Relational Somatic Psychotherapy*, which can be found at Bioenergetic Press.

His office address is:
150 Paularino Avenue #185
Costa Mesa, Ca. 92626

# Invitation to the IIBA 21ˢᵗ International Conference

## October 26–29, 2011, San Diego

*Diana Guest*

The conference committee would like to encourage you to come to the IIBA 21ˢᵗ International Conference to be held in beautiful San Diego, California. The Scientific Committee has put together a very exciting program. Daniel Siegel, MD is one of our keynote speakers. He is well known for his work with integrating mindfulness, neuroscience and psychotherapy. He has authored many books. Additionally, from Germany, we have Professor Joachim Bauer who will give us two talks on *"The Impact of Relational Experience on Genes" and "Mirror Neurons as a Neurological Basis for Intuition"*. We also have Helen Resnick-Sannes, PhD, CBT speaking on *"Recent findings in Neuroscience and their impact on our understanding of Attunement, Arousal and Affect."* This is just the start and the keynotes will be translated into 5 languages. We have more panels, demonstrations, bioenergetic exercises, affinity groups and rich afternoon workshops. We also have excellent pre-conference workshops you can sign up for. We have presenters from every region with a variety of languages and a few surprises in store for you. This is a great time to come together to appreciate the richness and knowledge of our global community.

For our North American attendees we have applied and hopefully by now been granted CEUs for the conference.

The Bahia Hotel is located less than 10 minutes from Lindbergh International Airport (a short taxi ride) and is on a private beach. It has several restaurants on the premises and there are also many restaurants, a roller coaster and public beaches within walking distance. To take a closer look at the hotel go to www.bahiahotel.com.

San Diego has much to offer as well. We have the 3rd largest city park, Balboa Park, in the U.S. with a number of museums, a phenomenal zoo, an outdoor organ pavilion as well as beautiful park grounds. We also have other attractions like Sea World, Legoland (for the kid in us), the Wild Animal Park, a Maritime Museum, the Gaslamp District and many other parks for hiking and of course our beautiful beaches and beautiful weather.

Hope to see you there!

*Diana Guest, BOT Liaison and Conference Chair*
*Alex Monroe, Scientific Committee Chair*
*Jan Parker, Logistics Committee Chair*
*Judy Silvan, CEU Committee Chair*

# Einladung zur 21. Internationalen IIBA-Konferenz

## 26.–29. Oktober 2011, San Diego

*Diana Guest*

Das Tagungskommittee lädt ein zur Teilnahme an der 21. Internationalen Konferenz in San Diego, Kalifornien. Die Wissenschaftskommission hat ein sehr spannendes Programm zusammen gestellt. Einen der Hauptvorträge wird Dr. med. Daniel Siegel halten. Er ist bekannt für seine Bemühungen, Achtsamkeit, Neurowissenschaften und Psychotherapie miteinander zu verbinden; er ist Autor vieler Bücher. Außerdem wird Prof. Dr. Joachim Bauer aus Deutschland zwei Vorträge halten: *"Gene als biologische Kommunikatoren – Auswirkungen von Beziehungserfahrungen auf die Aktivität unserer Gene"* und *"Spiegelneurone als eine neurobiologische Grundlage von Intuition"*. Darüber hinaus wird Dr. phil. Helen Resneck-Sannes, CBT, über *"Neuere neurowissenschaftliche Forschungsergebnisse und deren Auswirkung auf unser Verständnis von Attunement, Erregung und Affekten"* referieren. Die Hauptvorträge werden in 5 Sprachen übersetzt. Zusätzlich wird es Diskussionsrunden, Demonstrationen, Übungsgruppen, Gesprächsgruppen und eine reichhaltige Auswahl an Nachmittagsworkshops geben. Wir bieten interessante Präkonferenz-Workshops an, für die man sich extra anmelden kann. Es erwarten Sie Vortragende aus allen Regionen, die unterschiedliche Sprachen sprechen und außerdem einige Überraschungen. Dies ist eine großartige Gelegenheit, zusammen zu kommen und den Reichtum und das Wissen unserer globalen Gemeinschaft zu würdigen.

Für unsere nordamerikanischen TeilnehmerInnen haben wir uns um

CEUs (Weiterbildungskreditpunkte) beworben und hoffen, dass uns diese inzwischen bewilligt wurden.

Das Hotel Bahia liegt weniger als 10 Minuten vom Internationalen Flughafen Lindbergh entfernt (eine kurze Taxifahrt) und verfügt über einen Privatstrand. Zum Hotelkomplex gehören mehrere Restaurants. Zu Fuß erreichbar sind weitere Eßlokale, eine Achterbahn, sowie öffentliche Strände. Zur näheren Information, siehe www.bahiahotel.com.

San Diego hat viel zu bieten. Es umfasst den drittgrößten Stadtpark, Balboa Park, der Vereinigten Staaten, mit mehreren Museen, einem phänomenalen Zoo, einem "Outdoor Organ Pavillion", ebenso wie wunderschönen Parkflächen. Weitere Attraktionen sind das "Sea World", Legoland (für die Kinder in uns), der Wildtierpark, ein Meeresmuseum, der Gaslampen-Bezirk, viele Wandermöglichkeiten und natürlich die herrlichen Strände und das wunderschöne Wetter.

Wir hoffen, Sie hier begrüßen zu dürfen!

*Diana Guest, Kontaktperson zum Board of Trustees und Konferenzvorsitz*
*Alex Monroe, Präsident der Wissenschaftskommission*
*Jan Parker, Präsidentin der Logistikkommission*
*Judy Silvan, Präsidentin der CEU-Kommission*

# IIBA 21ᵉᵐᵉ Conference Internationale

## 26–29 Octobre 2011, San Diego

*Diana Guest*

Le comité de la conférence souhaiterait vous encourager à venir à la 21ᵉᵐᵉ conférence internationale qui aura lieu dans la très belle ville de San Diego, Californie, USA. Le Comité scientifique a mis en place un programme très enthousiasmant. Daniel Siegel, MD, est un des conférenciers principaux. Il est bien connu pour son travail sur l'intégration de la conscience, des neurosciences et de la psychothérapie. Il est l'auteur de beaucoup de livres. De plus, venant d'Allemagne, nous avons le Professeur Bauer qui nous fera deux interventions sur *"L'impact de l'Expérience Relationnelle sur les Gènes"* et *"Les Neurones Miroirs comme base en tant que base Neurologique de l'Intuition"* Nous avons également Helen Resnick-Sannes PHD, CBT, qui parlera des *"Découvertes récentes en Neuroscience et leur impact sur notre compréhension de l'Accordage, l'Excitation et l'Emotion"*. Ceci n'est que le début, les conférences principales seront traduites en cinq langues. Nous avons plus de panels, démonstrations, exercices bioénergétiques, groupes d'affinité et ateliers enrichissants l'après-midi. Nous avons également d'excellents séminaires de pré-conférence auxquels vous pouvez vous inscrire. Nous avons des présentateurs de chaque région avec une variété de langues et quelques surprises en réserve pour vous. Ceci est une grande occasion de nous retrouver afin d'apprécier la richesse et les connaissances de l'ensemble de notre communauté.

Pour nos assistants nord-américains nous avons demandé et espérons avoir à présent obtenu des CEU pour la conférence.

L'Hôtel Bahia est situé à moins de dix minutes de l'Aéroport International Lindbergh (une courte course en taxi) et sur une plage privée. Quelques restaurants se trouvent sur les lieux, il y a également beaucoup d'autres restaurants, un grand huit et des plages publiques à portée de pieds. Pour avoir une meilleure vue de l'hôtel aller à www.bahiahotel. com.

San Diego a également beaucoup à offrir. Nous avons le troisième plus grand parc de la ville aux Etats-Unis, Balboa Park, un grand nombre de musées, un zoo phénoménal, un kiosque à orgue, ainsi que des parcs magnifiques. Nous avons également d'autres attractions comme le Sea World, Lego Land (pour l'enfant à l'intérieur de nous), le Parc d'Animaux Sauvages, un Musée Maritime, le District Gaslamp, et beaucoup d'autres parcs pour randonnées et bien entendu nos très belles plages et un excellent climat.

En souhaitant vous y voir.

*Diana Guest, BOT liaison et Présidente de la Conférence*
*Alex Monroe, Président du Comité Scientifique*
*Jan Parker, Président du Comité Logistique*
*Judy Silvan, Président du Comité CEU*

# 21º Congreso Internacional del IIBA

## 26–29 de Octubre, 2011, San Diego

*Diana Guest*

El Comité del Congreso quiere animaros a asistir al 21º Congreso Internacional del IIBA que tendrá lugar en San Diego, California. El Comité Científico ha preparado un programa muy estimulante. Daniel Siegel, MD es uno de nuestros ponentes principales. Es ampliamente conocido por su trabajo integrativo de conciencia, neurociencia y psicoterapia. Es autor de muchos libros. Además, desde Alemania, tendremos al profesor Joaquim Bauer que presentaré dos ponencias: "El Impacto de la Experiencia Relacional en los Genes" y "Las Neuronas Espejo como Base Neurológica para la Intuición". También contaremos con Helen Resnick-Sannes, Phd, CBT, cuya ponencia versará sobre, "Descubrimientos recientes en Neurociencia y su impacto en nuestra comprensión de la Empatía, el Movimiento y la Emoción". Esto es solo el principio y las ponencias principales serán traducidas a cinco idiomas. Tenemos paneles, demostraciones, ejercicios bioenergéticos, grupos de afinidad e interesantes talleres por las tardes. También tendremos excelentes talleres pre-congreso a los que os podéis inscribir. Habrá ponentes de cada región con una variedad de lenguajes y unas cuantas sorpresas preparadas para vosotros/as. Es una muy buena ocasión para encontrarnos y apreciar la riqueza de conocimiento de nuestra comunidad global.

Para nuestros asistentes norteamericanos hemos pedido y se nos ha concedido créditos CEUs para el Congreso.

El hotel Bahia está situado a menos de 10 minutos del Aeropuerto Internacional Lindberg (un viaje corto en taxi) y cuenta con una playa privada. Tiene varios restaurantes y hay muchos más restaurantes, playas públicas y un parque de atracciones a poca distancia andando. Podéis entrar en www.bahiahotel.com para mirar el hotel más detalladamente.

San Diego también tiene mucho que ofrecer. Tenemos el 3er parque urbano más extenso de los Estados Unidos, el Balboa Park, con varios museos, un zoo fantástico, un quiosco exterior con órgano así como bellos parajes. También tenemos otras atracciones tales como Sea World, Legoland (para el niño/a que llevamos dentro), el Wild Animal Park, el Maritime Museum, el Gaslamp District y muchos otros parques para hacer senderismo y desde luego, nuestras preciosas playas y fantástica temperatura.

Espero veros a todos/as allí¡

*Diana Guest, Miembro del BOT y Presidenta del Congreso*
*Alex Monroe, Presidente del Comité Científico*
*Jan Parker, Presidente del Comité de Organización*
*Judy Silvan, Presidente del Comité CEU*

# XXI Conferenza Internazionale dell'IIBA

## 26–29 Ottobre 2011, San Diego

*Diana Guest, MFT, CBT*

La Commissione per l'organizzazione della Conferenza invita tutti a partecipare alla XXI Conferenza Internazionale che si terrà in California, nella città di San Diego. Il Comitato Scientifico ha predisposto un programma molto interessante. Daniel Siegel, autore di molte opere e molto conosciuto per i suoi studi che integrano ricerca cognitiva, neuroscienze e psicoterapia sarà uno dei relatori principali. Il prof. Joachim Bauer, terrà due interventi sull' "Impatto dell'esperienza relazionale sui geni" e "Neuroni Specchio, base neurologica dell'intuizione" Helen Resnick-Sannes, PhD, CBT parlerà delle "Scoperte recenti delle neuroscienze e il loro impatto sulla nostra comprensione della sintonizzazione, dell'arousal e degli affetti". Le relazioni introduttive saranno tradotte in cinque lingue. Ci saranno tavole rotonde, dimostrazioni, esercizi bioenergetici, affinity group e pomeriggi con molti workshop. Sarà possibile iscriversi anche a degli interessanti workshop che precederanno l'inizio della Conferenza. Ci sono relatori e conduttori di workshop che vengono da ogni parte del mondo, che parlano lingue diverse e che hanno in serbo interessanti sorprese. Questa è un'ottima occasione per incontrarci ed apprezzare la ricchezza e la competenza della nostra comunità internazionale.

L'hotel Bahia è a meno di dieci minuti di auto dal Lindbergh International Airport, ha una spiaggia privata, numerosi ristoranti. Per avere più informazioni potete andare sul sito www.bahiahotel.com.

Anche San Diego ha molto da offrire. Abbiamo il terzo più grande parco cittadino degli Stati Uniti, il Balboa Park, con molti musei, un grande zoo e innumerevoli attrazioni culturali e sportive oltre ad un tempo piacevole che consente di godere delle spiagge.

Speriamo di incontrarvi qui!

*Diana Guest, Per i contatti con il BOT e Presidente della Conferenza*
*Alex Monroe, Presidente del Comitato Scientifico*
*Jan Parker, Presidente del Comitato Logistico*
*Judy Silvan, Presidente del CEU*

# 21º Congresso Internacional do IIBA

## 26–27 de Outubro de 2011

*Diana Guest, MFT, CBT*

O comitê executivo do congresso gostaria de reiterar o convite para que você venha ao 21º Congresso Internacional a ser realizada em San Diego, Califórnia. O Comitê Científico elaborou um programa fantástico. O Dr. Daniel Siegel será um dos palestrantes: ele é muito conhecido pelo seu trabalho que integra o estudo da mente, a Neurociência e a psicoterapia, alem de seu autor de diversos livros.

Outro convidado, vindo da Alemanha, é o Prof. Joachim Bauer, que fará duas palestras: "*O impacto da experiência emocional nos genes*" e "Neurônios-espelho como base neurológica para a intuição".

Teremos também Helen Resneck-Sannes, PhD, CBT, falando sobre "*Achados recentes em Neurociência e seu impacto em nossa compreensão da excitação, sintonia e afeto*". Isto é só o começo e todas as palestras magnas serão traduzidas em 5 línguas. Teremos ainda painéis, demonstrações, exercícios bioenergéticos, grupos de afinidade e tardes recheadas de workshops – além de apresentadores de todas as regiões com uma enorme variedade de idiomas e muitas surpresas reservadas para você. Há também excelentes workshops pré-congresso, para os quais você poderá se inscrever. É uma excelente oportunidade de nos reunirmos para aproveitar a riqueza e o conhecimento de nossa comunidade global.

Para os participantes da América do Norte, solicitamos – e espero, a esta altura, termos conseguido CEUs para o congresso.

O Hotel Bahia está localizado a menos de 10 minutos do Aeroporto Internacional de Lindbergh (a uma curta corrida de táxi) e é dotado de praia particular. Há vários restaurantes em suas dependências, assim como há muitos restaurantes, uma montanha russa e praias públicas a uma curta distância á pé. Para dar uma olhada no hotel, vá ao site: www. bahiahotel.com.

San Diego também tem muito a oferecer. Temos o 3º maior parque dos USA, o Parque Balboa, com vários museus e um zoológico fenomenal, e também outros parques. Pode-se encontrar também outras atrações: O Sea World, a Legoland (para a criança dentro de nós ...), o Wild Animal park, Museu Marítimo, a Gaslamp District e várias outras atrações – além de nosso clima maravilhoso!

Esperamos vê-lo lá!

*Diana Guest, liaison do BOT e Presidente do Congresso*
*Alex Monroe, presidente do Comitê Científico*
*Jan Parker, Presidente do Comitê de Logística*
*Judy Silvan, presidente do Comitê CEU*

Hans-Jürgen Wirth

## 9/11 as a Collective Trauma

### and other Essays on Psychoanalysis and Society

Hans-Jürgen Wirth

## Narcissism and Power

### Psychoanalysis of Mental Disorders in Politics

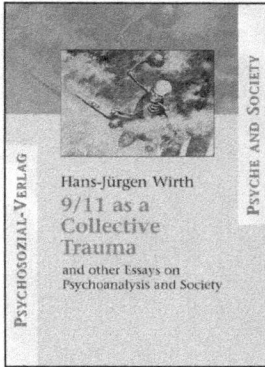

*2004 · 198 pages · hardback*
*ISBN 978-3-89806-372-2*

*2009 · 266 pages · hardback*
*ISBN 978-3-89806-480-4*

In 9/11 as a Collective Trauma Hans-Jürgen Wirth presents a collection of his most interesting essays about psyche and politics. He reflects on the psychic structure of suicide bombers and analyzes the psycho-political causes and the consequences of the Iraq War. The other essays focus on xenophobia and violence, the story of Jewish psychoanalysts who emigrated to the United States from Nazi Germany, and the idea of man in psychoanalysis.

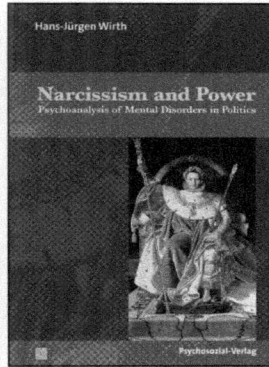

Social power is irresistibly appealing to narcissistically disturbed personalities. Uninhibited egocentricity, career obsession, a winning mentality and fantasies of grandeur – the narcissist employs these traits to clear the way through the corridors of economic and political power.

Blinded by his fantasies of grandeur and omnipotence, the narcissist loses his grasp on social reality and necessarily fails in the end. It is closely related to this loss of reality that the leader turns away from the norms, values and ideals to which he should actually be committed. Obsession with power, unscrupulousness and cynicism can give rise to brutal misanthropy.

Walltorstr. 10 · 35390 Giessen · Phone +49 641-96 99 78-18 · Fax +49 641-96 99 78-19
bestellung@psychosozial-verlag.de · www.psychosozial-verlag.de

Ralf Vogt

## »Beseelbare« Therapy Objects

**Psychoanalytic interactional approach in a body- and trauma-oriented psychotherapy**

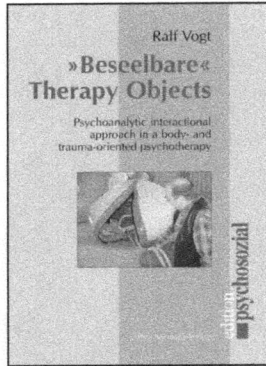

Ralf Vogt

## Psychotrauma, State, Setting

**Psychoanalytical-Action-Related Model for a Treatment of Complexly Traumatized Patients (SPIM-20-CTP)**

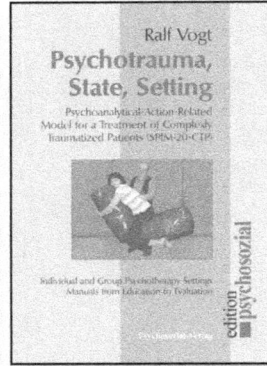

*2006 · 187 pages · paperback*
*ISBN 978-3-89806-700-3*

*2008 · 337 pages · paperback*
*ISBN 978-3-89806-871-0*

Ralf Vogt presents a new form of body therapy which may be applied as individual and as group psychotherapy. The core of his original concept are »»beseelbare‹ objects«. With the help of such objects, typical conflict situations may be performed and problem-specific solutions may be playfully tested. The objects used to that end – for example a cuddly cave into which the patient may crawl – were specifically designed for psychotherapeutic work by the author. These »»beseelbare‹ therapy objects« are an important aid to get access to any blocked or buried affects of the patients.

Ralf Vogt presents a complete conception of a psychotraumatological treatment which is applicable to complex traumatized patients (representing the majority of psychotrauma disorders in ambulant practices) as well as to other patients. His very structured procedure with theoretical derivations, including many handouts for clients and treaters, and specific case vignettes, is unique and important in its compactness to the point of evaluation. The book is suitable reading for therapists and advisors, and also for advanced patients.

Walltorstr. 10 · 35390 Giessen · Phone +49 641-96 99 78-18 · Fax +49 641-96 99 78-19
bestellung@psychosozial-verlag.de · www.psychosozial-verlag.de